C-3670　　CAREER EXAMINATION SERIES

This is your
PASSBOOK for...

Campus Peace Officer

Test Preparation Study Guide
Questions & Answers

COPYRIGHT NOTICE

This book is SOLELY intended for, is sold ONLY to, and its use is RESTRICTED to individual, bona fide applicants or candidates who qualify by virtue of having seriously filed applications for appropriate license, certificate, professional and/or promotional advancement, higher school matriculation, scholarship, or other legitimate requirements of education and/or governmental authorities.

This book is NOT intended for use, class instruction, tutoring, training, duplication, copying, reprinting, excerption, or adaptation, etc., by:

1) Other publishers
2) Proprietors and/or Instructors of "Coaching" and/or Preparatory Courses
3) Personnel and/or Training Divisions of commercial, industrial, and governmental organizations
4) Schools, colleges, or universities and/or their departments and staffs, including teachers and other personnel
5) Testing Agencies or Bureaus
6) Study groups which seek by the purchase of a single volume to copy and/or duplicate and/or adapt this material for use by the group as a whole without having purchased individual volumes for each of the members of the group
7) Et al.

Such persons would be in violation of appropriate Federal and State statutes.

PROVISION OF LICENSING AGREEMENTS – Recognized educational, commercial, industrial, and governmental institutions and organizations, and others legitimately engaged in educational pursuits, including training, testing, and measurement activities, may address request for a licensing agreement to the copyright owners, who will determine whether, and under what conditions, including fees and charges, the materials in this book may be used them. In other words, a licensing facility exists for the legitimate use of the material in this book on other than an individual basis. However, it is asseverated and affirmed here that the material in this book CANNOT be used without the receipt of the express permission of such a licensing agreement from the Publishers. Inquiries re licensing should be addressed to the company, attention rights and permissions department.

All rights reserved, including the right of reproduction in whole or in part, in any form or by any means, electronic or mechanical, including photocopying, recording, or by any information storage and retrieval system, without permission in writing from the Publisher.

Copyright © 2025 by
National Learning Corporation

212 Michael Drive, Syosset, NY 11791
(516) 921-8888 • www.passbooks.com
E-mail: info@passbooks.com

PASSBOOK® SERIES

THE *PASSBOOK® SERIES* has been created to prepare applicants and candidates for the ultimate academic battlefield – the examination room.

At some time in our lives, each and every one of us may be required to take an examination – for validation, matriculation, admission, qualification, registration, certification, or licensure.

Based on the assumption that every applicant or candidate has met the basic formal educational standards, has taken the required number of courses, and read the necessary texts, the *PASSBOOK® SERIES* furnishes the one special preparation which may assure passing with confidence, instead of failing with insecurity. Examination questions – together with answers – are furnished as the basic vehicle for study so that the mysteries of the examination and its compounding difficulties may be eliminated or diminished by a sure method.

This book is meant to help you pass your examination provided that you qualify and are serious in your objective.

The entire field is reviewed through the huge store of content information which is succinctly presented through a provocative and challenging approach – the question-and-answer method.

A climate of success is established by furnishing the correct answers at the end of each test.

You soon learn to recognize types of questions, forms of questions, and patterns of questioning. You may even begin to anticipate expected outcomes.

You perceive that many questions are repeated or adapted so that you can gain acute insights, which may enable you to score many sure points.

You learn how to confront new questions, or types of questions, and to attack them confidently and work out the correct answers.

You note objectives and emphases, and recognize pitfalls and dangers, so that you may make positive educational adjustments.

Moreover, you are kept fully informed in relation to new concepts, methods, practices, and directions in the field.

You discover that you are actually taking the examination all the time: you are preparing for the examination by "taking" an examination, not by reading extraneous and/or supererogatory textbooks.

In short, this PASSBOOK®, used directedly, should be an important factor in helping you to pass your test.

CAMPUS PEACE OFFICER

DUTIES

Patrols city university campuses to maintain the peace and provide security for the) university, its buildings, educators and students. Performs related duties.

Officers also carry out the following general work tasks: respond to alarms and calls for service from members of the college community; enforce college rules and regulations as specified in Standard Operating Procedures; maintain a personal record (memo book) of daily job activities and incidents, as they occur, in the manner determined by the campus public safety director; maintain radio contact with the department's central dispatch to ensure proper campus surveillance and to help coordinate public safety operations; provide customer service to members of the college community and visitors; assist with crowd control at registration, special events and other functions; maintain and update post and tour logs; write complete and accurate reports to record campus incidents; escort students, college VIPs, visiting dignitaries and others on foot and/or college vehicles; investigate crimes applying departmental procedures, in accordance with all rules, regulations and applicable laws; use and maintain defensive equipment (e.g. ASP, handcuffs, pepper spray, etc.); make arrests, and perform arrest processing, according to departmental procedures and all relevant rules, regulations and laws; provide testimony in college disciplinary and legal proceedings; voucher evidence using established procedures; help monitor the performance of campus security assistants and security guards; carefully monitor the premises through campus closed-circuit television; perform assigned fire safety duties, such as fire drills, emergencies and other building evacuations; inventory public safety equipment; check IDs and parking passes/decals; provide authorized access to rooms and locations; accept and voucher items into Lost and Found; act as first responder to alarms and calls for service; conduct patrols of campus on foot and by driving marked, unmarked and cart vehicles; control the flow of vehicle and pedestrian traffic to ensure safety and security of persons and property; perform various driving details as assigned; and upon volunteering for and being selected; incumbents serve as members of special patrols, such as Bike, Canine and team patrol units.

SCOPE OF THE EXAMINATION

These questions test for general knowledge, skills and abilities of the principles and practices employed in performing the duties associated with the Campus Peace Officer position. The potential content areas include: judgment, observation, dispute resolution, customer service, interviewing, communication, listening, and ability to follow orders/take direction, organization, telephone, and writing skills. The test may consist of self-evaluation questions that assess applicants in the following areas: interpersonal skills; taking directions; work attitude, work ethic and reliability; motivation and personal initiative; stress tolerance; compassion and conscientiousness; and service orientation.

HOW TO TAKE A TEST

I. YOU MUST PASS AN EXAMINATION

A. *WHAT EVERY CANDIDATE SHOULD KNOW*

Examination applicants often ask us for help in preparing for the written test. What can I study in advance? What kinds of questions will be asked? How will the test be given? How will the papers be graded?

As an applicant for a civil service examination, you may be wondering about some of these things. Our purpose here is to suggest effective methods of advance study and to describe civil service examinations.

Your chances for success on this examination can be increased if you know how to prepare. Those "pre-examination jitters" can be reduced if you know what to expect. You can even experience an adventure in good citizenship if you know why civil service exams are given.

B. *WHY ARE CIVIL SERVICE EXAMINATIONS GIVEN?*

Civil service examinations are important to you in two ways. As a citizen, you want public jobs filled by employees who know how to do their work. As a job seeker, you want a fair chance to compete for that job on an equal footing with other candidates. The best-known means of accomplishing this two-fold goal is the competitive examination.

Exams are widely publicized throughout the nation. They may be administered for jobs in federal, state, city, municipal, town or village governments or agencies.

Any citizen may apply, with some limitations, such as the age or residence of applicants. Your experience and education may be reviewed to see whether you meet the requirements for the particular examination. When these requirements exist, they are reasonable and applied consistently to all applicants. Thus, a competitive examination may cause you some uneasiness now, but it is your privilege and safeguard.

C. *HOW ARE CIVIL SERVICE EXAMS DEVELOPED?*

Examinations are carefully written by trained technicians who are specialists in the field known as "psychological measurement," in consultation with recognized authorities in the field of work that the test will cover. These experts recommend the subject matter areas or skills to be tested; only those knowledges or skills important to your success on the job are included. The most reliable books and source materials available are used as references. Together, the experts and technicians judge the difficulty level of the questions.

Test technicians know how to phrase questions so that the problem is clearly stated. Their ethics do not permit "trick" or "catch" questions. Questions may have been tried out on sample groups, or subjected to statistical analysis, to determine their usefulness.

Written tests are often used in combination with performance tests, ratings of training and experience, and oral interviews. All of these measures combine to form the best-known means of finding the right person for the right job.

II. HOW TO PASS THE WRITTEN TEST

A. NATURE OF THE EXAMINATION

To prepare intelligently for civil service examinations, you should know how they differ from school examinations you have taken. In school you were assigned certain definite pages to read or subjects to cover. The examination questions were quite detailed and usually emphasized memory. Civil service exams, on the other hand, try to discover your present ability to perform the duties of a position, plus your potentiality to learn these duties. In other words, a civil service exam attempts to predict how successful you will be. Questions cover such a broad area that they cannot be as minute and detailed as school exam questions.

In the public service similar kinds of work, or positions, are grouped together in one "class." This process is known as *position-classification*. All the positions in a class are paid according to the salary range for that class. One class title covers all of these positions, and they are all tested by the same examination.

B. FOUR BASIC STEPS

1) Study the announcement

How, then, can you know what subjects to study? Our best answer is: "Learn as much as possible about the class of positions for which you've applied." The exam will test the knowledge, skills and abilities needed to do the work.

Your most valuable source of information about the position you want is the official exam announcement. This announcement lists the training and experience qualifications. Check these standards and apply only if you come reasonably close to meeting them.

The brief description of the position in the examination announcement offers some clues to the subjects which will be tested. Think about the job itself. Review the duties in your mind. Can you perform them, or are there some in which you are rusty? Fill in the blank spots in your preparation.

Many jurisdictions preview the written test in the exam announcement by including a section called "Knowledge and Abilities Required," "Scope of the Examination," or some similar heading. Here you will find out specifically what fields will be tested.

2) Review your own background

Once you learn in general what the position is all about, and what you need to know to do the work, ask yourself which subjects you already know fairly well and which need improvement. You may wonder whether to concentrate on improving your strong areas or on building some background in your fields of weakness. When the announcement has specified "some knowledge" or "considerable knowledge," or has used adjectives like "beginning principles of..." or "advanced ... methods," you can get a clue as to the number and difficulty of questions to be asked in any given field. More questions, and hence broader coverage, would be included for those subjects which are more important in the work. Now weigh your strengths and weaknesses against the job requirements and prepare accordingly.

3) Determine the level of the position

Another way to tell how intensively you should prepare is to understand the level of the job for which you are applying. Is it the entering level? In other words, is this the position in which beginners in a field of work are hired? Or is it an intermediate or advanced level? Sometimes this is indicated by such words as "Junior" or "Senior" in the class title. Other jurisdictions use Roman numerals to designate the level – Clerk I, Clerk II, for example. The word "Supervisor" sometimes appears in the title. If the level is not indicated by the title, check the description of duties. Will you be working under very close supervision, or will you have responsibility for independent decisions in this work?

4) Choose appropriate study materials

Now that you know the subjects to be examined and the relative amount of each subject to be covered, you can choose suitable study materials. For beginning level jobs, or even advanced ones, if you have a pronounced weakness in some aspect of your training, read a modern, standard textbook in that field. Be sure it is up to date and has general coverage. Such books are normally available at your library, and the librarian will be glad to help you locate one. For entry-level positions, questions of appropriate difficulty are chosen – neither highly advanced questions, nor those too simple. Such questions require careful thought but not advanced training.

If the position for which you are applying is technical or advanced, you will read more advanced, specialized material. If you are already familiar with the basic principles of your field, elementary textbooks would waste your time. Concentrate on advanced textbooks and technical periodicals. Think through the concepts and review difficult problems in your field.

These are all general sources. You can get more ideas on your own initiative, following these leads. For example, training manuals and publications of the government agency which employs workers in your field can be useful, particularly for technical and professional positions. A letter or visit to the government department involved may result in more specific study suggestions, and certainly will provide you with a more definite idea of the exact nature of the position you are seeking.

III. KINDS OF TESTS

Tests are used for purposes other than measuring knowledge and ability to perform specified duties. For some positions, it is equally important to test ability to make adjustments to new situations or to profit from training. In others, basic mental abilities not dependent on information are essential. Questions which test these things may not appear as pertinent to the duties of the position as those which test for knowledge and information. Yet they are often highly important parts of a fair examination. For very general questions, it is almost impossible to help you direct your study efforts. What we can do is to point out some of the more common of these general abilities needed in public service positions and describe some typical questions.

1) General information

Broad, general information has been found useful for predicting job success in some kinds of work. This is tested in a variety of ways, from vocabulary lists to questions about current events. Basic background in some field of work, such as sociology or economics, may be sampled in a group of questions. Often these are principles which have become familiar to most persons through exposure rather than through formal training. It is difficult to advise you how to study for these questions; being alert to the world around you is our best suggestion.

2) Verbal ability

An example of an ability needed in many positions is verbal or language ability. Verbal ability is, in brief, the ability to use and understand words. Vocabulary and grammar tests are typical measures of this ability. Reading comprehension or paragraph interpretation questions are common in many kinds of civil service tests. You are given a paragraph of written material and asked to find its central meaning.

3) Numerical ability
Number skills can be tested by the familiar arithmetic problem, by checking paired lists of numbers to see which are alike and which are different, or by interpreting charts and graphs. In the latter test, a graph may be printed in the test booklet which you are asked to use as the basis for answering questions.

4) Observation
A popular test for law-enforcement positions is the observation test. A picture is shown to you for several minutes, then taken away. Questions about the picture test your ability to observe both details and larger elements.

5) Following directions
In many positions in the public service, the employee must be able to carry out written instructions dependably and accurately. You may be given a chart with several columns, each column listing a variety of information. The questions require you to carry out directions involving the information given in the chart.

6) Skills and aptitudes
Performance tests effectively measure some manual skills and aptitudes. When the skill is one in which you are trained, such as typing or shorthand, you can practice. These tests are often very much like those given in business school or high school courses. For many of the other skills and aptitudes, however, no short-time preparation can be made. Skills and abilities natural to you or that you have developed throughout your lifetime are being tested.

Many of the general questions just described provide all the data needed to answer the questions and ask you to use your reasoning ability to find the answers. Your best preparation for these tests, as well as for tests of facts and ideas, is to be at your physical and mental best. You, no doubt, have your own methods of getting into an exam-taking mood and keeping "in shape." The next section lists some ideas on this subject.

IV. KINDS OF QUESTIONS

Only rarely is the "essay" question, which you answer in narrative form, used in civil service tests. Civil service tests are usually of the short-answer type. Full instructions for answering these questions will be given to you at the examination. But in case this is your first experience with short-answer questions and separate answer sheets, here is what you need to know:

1) Multiple-choice Questions
Most popular of the short-answer questions is the "multiple choice" or "best answer" question. It can be used, for example, to test for factual knowledge, ability to solve problems or judgment in meeting situations found at work.
A multiple-choice question is normally one of three types—
- It can begin with an incomplete statement followed by several possible endings. You are to find the one ending which *best* completes the statement, although some of the others may not be entirely wrong.
- It can also be a complete statement in the form of a question which is answered by choosing one of the statements listed.

- It can be in the form of a problem – again you select the best answer.

Here is an example of a multiple-choice question with a discussion which should give you some clues as to the method for choosing the right answer:

When an employee has a complaint about his assignment, the action which will *best* help him overcome his difficulty is to
   A. discuss his difficulty with his coworkers
   B. take the problem to the head of the organization
   C. take the problem to the person who gave him the assignment
   D. say nothing to anyone about his complaint

In answering this question, you should study each of the choices to find which is best. Consider choice "A" – Certainly an employee may discuss his complaint with fellow employees, but no change or improvement can result, and the complaint remains unresolved. Choice "B" is a poor choice since the head of the organization probably does not know what assignment you have been given, and taking your problem to him is known as "going over the head" of the supervisor. The supervisor, or person who made the assignment, is the person who can clarify it or correct any injustice. Choice "C" is, therefore, correct. To say nothing, as in choice "D," is unwise. Supervisors have and interest in knowing the problems employees are facing, and the employee is seeking a solution to his problem.

2) True/False Questions

The "true/false" or "right/wrong" form of question is sometimes used. Here a complete statement is given. Your job is to decide whether the statement is right or wrong.

SAMPLE: A roaming cell-phone call to a nearby city costs less than a non-roaming call to a distant city.

This statement is wrong, or false, since roaming calls are more expensive.

This is not a complete list of all possible question forms, although most of the others are variations of these common types. You will always get complete directions for answering questions. Be sure you understand *how* to mark your answers – ask questions until you do.

V. RECORDING YOUR ANSWERS

Computer terminals are used more and more today for many different kinds of exams.

For an examination with very few applicants, you may be told to record your answers in the test booklet itself. Separate answer sheets are much more common. If this separate answer sheet is to be scored by machine – and this is often the case – it is highly important that you mark your answers correctly in order to get credit.

An electronic scoring machine is often used in civil service offices because of the speed with which papers can be scored. Machine-scored answer sheets must be marked with a pencil, which will be given to you. This pencil has a high graphite content which responds to the electronic scoring machine. As a matter of fact, stray dots may register as answers, so do not let your pencil rest on the answer sheet while you are pondering the correct answer. Also, if your pencil lead breaks or is otherwise defective, ask for another.

Since the answer sheet will be dropped in a slot in the scoring machine, be careful not to bend the corners or get the paper crumpled.

The answer sheet normally has five vertical columns of numbers, with 30 numbers to a column. These numbers correspond to the question numbers in your test booklet. After each number, going across the page are four or five pairs of dotted lines. These short dotted lines have small letters or numbers above them. The first two pairs may also have a "T" or "F" above the letters. This indicates that the first two pairs only are to be used if the questions are of the true-false type. If the questions are multiple choice, disregard the "T" and "F" and pay attention only to the small letters or numbers.

Answer your questions in the manner of the sample that follows:

32. The largest city in the United States is
    A. Washington, D.C.
    B. New York City
    C. Chicago
    D. Detroit
    E. San Francisco

1) Choose the answer you think is best. (New York City is the largest, so "B" is correct.)
2) Find the row of dotted lines numbered the same as the question you are answering. (Find row number 32)
3) Find the pair of dotted lines corresponding to the answer. (Find the pair of lines under the mark "B.")
4) Make a solid black mark between the dotted lines.

VI. BEFORE THE TEST

Common sense will help you find procedures to follow to get ready for an examination. Too many of us, however, overlook these sensible measures. Indeed, nervousness and fatigue have been found to be the most serious reasons why applicants fail to do their best on civil service tests. Here is a list of reminders:

- Begin your preparation early – Don't wait until the last minute to go scurrying around for books and materials or to find out what the position is all about.
- Prepare continuously – An hour a night for a week is better than an all-night cram session. This has been definitely established. What is more, a night a week for a month will return better dividends than crowding your study into a shorter period of time.
- Locate the place of the exam – You have been sent a notice telling you when and where to report for the examination. If the location is in a different town or otherwise unfamiliar to you, it would be well to inquire the best route and learn something about the building.
- Relax the night before the test – Allow your mind to rest. Do not study at all that night. Plan some mild recreation or diversion; then go to bed early and get a good night's sleep.
- Get up early enough to make a leisurely trip to the place for the test – This way unforeseen events, traffic snarls, unfamiliar buildings, etc. will not upset you.
- Dress comfortably – A written test is not a fashion show. You will be known by number and not by name, so wear something comfortable.

- Leave excess paraphernalia at home – Shopping bags and odd bundles will get in your way. You need bring only the items mentioned in the official notice you received; usually everything you need is provided. Do not bring reference books to the exam. They will only confuse those last minutes and be taken away from you when in the test room.
- Arrive somewhat ahead of time – If because of transportation schedules you must get there very early, bring a newspaper or magazine to take your mind off yourself while waiting.
- Locate the examination room – When you have found the proper room, you will be directed to the seat or part of the room where you will sit. Sometimes you are given a sheet of instructions to read while you are waiting. Do not fill out any forms until you are told to do so; just read them and be prepared.
- Relax and prepare to listen to the instructions
- If you have any physical problem that may keep you from doing your best, be sure to tell the test administrator. If you are sick or in poor health, you really cannot do your best on the exam. You can come back and take the test some other time.

VII. AT THE TEST

The day of the test is here and you have the test booklet in your hand. The temptation to get going is very strong. Caution! There is more to success than knowing the right answers. You must know how to identify your papers and understand variations in the type of short-answer question used in this particular examination. Follow these suggestions for maximum results from your efforts:

1) Cooperate with the monitor

The test administrator has a duty to create a situation in which you can be as much at ease as possible. He will give instructions, tell you when to begin, check to see that you are marking your answer sheet correctly, and so on. He is not there to guard you, although he will see that your competitors do not take unfair advantage. He wants to help you do your best.

2) Listen to all instructions

Don't jump the gun! Wait until you understand all directions. In most civil service tests you get more time than you need to answer the questions. So don't be in a hurry. Read each word of instructions until you clearly understand the meaning. Study the examples, listen to all announcements and follow directions. Ask questions if you do not understand what to do.

3) Identify your papers

Civil service exams are usually identified by number only. You will be assigned a number; you must not put your name on your test papers. Be sure to copy your number correctly. Since more than one exam may be given, copy your exact examination title.

4) Plan your time

Unless you are told that a test is a "speed" or "rate of work" test, speed itself is usually not important. Time enough to answer all the questions will be provided, but this does not mean that you have all day. An overall time limit has been set. Divide the total time (in minutes) by the number of questions to determine the approximate time you have for each question.

5) Do not linger over difficult questions

If you come across a difficult question, mark it with a paper clip (useful to have along) and come back to it when you have been through the booklet. One caution if you do this – be sure to skip a number on your answer sheet as well. Check often to be sure that you have not lost your place and that you are marking in the row numbered the same as the question you are answering.

6) Read the questions

Be sure you know what the question asks! Many capable people are unsuccessful because they failed to *read* the questions correctly.

7) Answer all questions

Unless you have been instructed that a penalty will be deducted for incorrect answers, it is better to guess than to omit a question.

8) Speed tests

It is often better NOT to guess on speed tests. It has been found that on timed tests people are tempted to spend the last few seconds before time is called in marking answers at random – without even reading them – in the hope of picking up a few extra points. To discourage this practice, the instructions may warn you that your score will be "corrected" for guessing. That is, a penalty will be applied. The incorrect answers will be deducted from the correct ones, or some other penalty formula will be used.

9) Review your answers

If you finish before time is called, go back to the questions you guessed or omitted to give them further thought. Review other answers if you have time.

10) Return your test materials

If you are ready to leave before others have finished or time is called, take ALL your materials to the monitor and leave quietly. Never take any test material with you. The monitor can discover whose papers are not complete, and taking a test booklet may be grounds for disqualification.

VIII. EXAMINATION TECHNIQUES

1) Read the general instructions carefully. These are usually printed on the first page of the exam booklet. As a rule, these instructions refer to the timing of the examination; the fact that you should not start work until the signal and must stop work at a signal, etc. If there are any *special* instructions, such as a choice of questions to be answered, make sure that you note this instruction carefully.

2) When you are ready to start work on the examination, that is as soon as the signal has been given, read the instructions to each question booklet, underline any key words or phrases, such as *least, best, outline, describe* and the like. In this way you will tend to answer as requested rather than discover on reviewing your paper that you *listed without describing*, that you selected the *worst* choice rather than the *best* choice, etc.

3) If the examination is of the objective or multiple-choice type – that is, each question will also give a series of possible answers: A, B, C or D, and you are called upon to select the best answer and write the letter next to that answer on your answer paper – it is advisable to start answering each question in turn. There may be anywhere from 50 to 100 such questions in the three or four hours allotted and you can see how much time would be taken if you read through all the questions before beginning to answer any. Furthermore, if you come across a question or group of questions which you know would be difficult to answer, it would undoubtedly affect your handling of all the other questions.

4) If the examination is of the essay type and contains but a few questions, it is a moot point as to whether you should read all the questions before starting to answer any one. Of course, if you are given a choice – say five out of seven and the like – then it is essential to read all the questions so you can eliminate the two that are most difficult. If, however, you are asked to answer all the questions, there may be danger in trying to answer the easiest one first because you may find that you will spend too much time on it. The best technique is to answer the first question, then proceed to the second, etc.

5) Time your answers. Before the exam begins, write down the time it started, then add the time allowed for the examination and write down the time it must be completed, then divide the time available somewhat as follows:
    - If 3-1/2 hours are allowed, that would be 210 minutes. If you have 80 objective-type questions, that would be an average of 2-1/2 minutes per question. Allow yourself no more than 2 minutes per question, or a total of 160 minutes, which will permit about 50 minutes to review.
    - If for the time allotment of 210 minutes there are 7 essay questions to answer, that would average about 30 minutes a question. Give yourself only 25 minutes per question so that you have about 35 minutes to review.

6) The most important instruction is to *read each question* and make sure you know what is wanted. The second most important instruction is to *time yourself properly* so that you answer every question. The third most important instruction is to *answer every question*. Guess if you have to but include something for each question. Remember that you will receive no credit for a blank and will probably receive some credit if you write something in answer to an essay question. If you guess a letter – say "B" for a multiple-choice question – you may have guessed right. If you leave a blank as an answer to a multiple-choice question, the examiners may respect your feelings but it will not add a point to your score. Some exams may penalize you for wrong answers, so in such cases *only*, you may not want to guess unless you have some basis for your answer.

7) Suggestions
    a. Objective-type questions
        1. Examine the question booklet for proper sequence of pages and questions
        2. Read all instructions carefully
        3. Skip any question which seems too difficult; return to it after all other questions have been answered
        4. Apportion your time properly; do not spend too much time on any single question or group of questions

5. Note and underline key words – *all, most, fewest, least, best, worst, same, opposite,* etc.
6. Pay particular attention to negatives
7. Note unusual option, e.g., unduly long, short, complex, different or similar in content to the body of the question
8. Observe the use of "hedging" words – *probably, may, most likely,* etc.
9. Make sure that your answer is put next to the same number as the question
10. Do not second-guess unless you have good reason to believe the second answer is definitely more correct
11. Cross out original answer if you decide another answer is more accurate; do not erase until you are ready to hand your paper in
12. Answer all questions; guess unless instructed otherwise
13. Leave time for review

   b. Essay questions
   1. Read each question carefully
   2. Determine exactly what is wanted. Underline key words or phrases.
   3. Decide on outline or paragraph answer
   4. Include many different points and elements unless asked to develop any one or two points or elements
   5. Show impartiality by giving pros and cons unless directed to select one side only
   6. Make and write down any assumptions you find necessary to answer the questions
   7. Watch your English, grammar, punctuation and choice of words
   8. Time your answers; don't crowd material

8) Answering the essay question

Most essay questions can be answered by framing the specific response around several key words or ideas. Here are a few such key words or ideas:

M's: manpower, materials, methods, money, management
P's: purpose, program, policy, plan, procedure, practice, problems, pitfalls, personnel, public relations

   a. Six basic steps in handling problems:
   1. Preliminary plan and background development
   2. Collect information, data and facts
   3. Analyze and interpret information, data and facts
   4. Analyze and develop solutions as well as make recommendations
   5. Prepare report and sell recommendations
   6. Install recommendations and follow up effectiveness

   b. Pitfalls to avoid
   1. *Taking things for granted* – A statement of the situation does not necessarily imply that each of the elements is necessarily true; for example, a complaint may be invalid and biased so that all that can be taken for granted is that a complaint has been registered

2. *Considering only one side of a situation* – Wherever possible, indicate several alternatives and then point out the reasons you selected the best one
3. *Failing to indicate follow up* – Whenever your answer indicates action on your part, make certain that you will take proper follow-up action to see how successful your recommendations, procedures or actions turn out to be
4. *Taking too long in answering any single question* – Remember to time your answers properly

IX. AFTER THE TEST

Scoring procedures differ in detail among civil service jurisdictions although the general principles are the same. Whether the papers are hand-scored or graded by machine we have described, they are nearly always graded by number. That is, the person who marks the paper knows only the number – never the name – of the applicant. Not until all the papers have been graded will they be matched with names. If other tests, such as training and experience or oral interview ratings have been given, scores will be combined. Different parts of the examination usually have different weights. For example, the written test might count 60 percent of the final grade, and a rating of training and experience 40 percent. In many jurisdictions, veterans will have a certain number of points added to their grades.

After the final grade has been determined, the names are placed in grade order and an eligible list is established. There are various methods for resolving ties between those who get the same final grade – probably the most common is to place first the name of the person whose application was received first. Job offers are made from the eligible list in the order the names appear on it. You will be notified of your grade and your rank as soon as all these computations have been made. This will be done as rapidly as possible.

People who are found to meet the requirements in the announcement are called "eligibles." Their names are put on a list of eligible candidates. An eligible's chances of getting a job depend on how high he stands on this list and how fast agencies are filling jobs from the list.

When a job is to be filled from a list of eligibles, the agency asks for the names of people on the list of eligibles for that job. When the civil service commission receives this request, it sends to the agency the names of the three people highest on this list. Or, if the job to be filled has specialized requirements, the office sends the agency the names of the top three persons who meet these requirements from the general list.

The appointing officer makes a choice from among the three people whose names were sent to him. If the selected person accepts the appointment, the names of the others are put back on the list to be considered for future openings.

That is the rule in hiring from all kinds of eligible lists, whether they are for typist, carpenter, chemist, or something else. For every vacancy, the appointing officer has his choice of any one of the top three eligibles on the list. This explains why the person whose name is on top of the list sometimes does not get an appointment when some of the persons lower on the list do. If the appointing officer chooses the second or third eligible, the No. 1 eligible does not get a job at once, but stays on the list until he is appointed or the list is terminated.

X. HOW TO PASS THE INTERVIEW TEST

The examination for which you applied requires an oral interview test. You have already taken the written test and you are now being called for the interview test – the final part of the formal examination.

You may think that it is not possible to prepare for an interview test and that there are no procedures to follow during an interview. Our purpose is to point out some things you can do in advance that will help you and some good rules to follow and pitfalls to avoid while you are being interviewed.

What is an interview supposed to test?

The written examination is designed to test the technical knowledge and competence of the candidate; the oral is designed to evaluate intangible qualities, not readily measured otherwise, and to establish a list showing the relative fitness of each candidate – as measured against his competitors – for the position sought. Scoring is not on the basis of "right" and "wrong," but on a sliding scale of values ranging from "not passable" to "outstanding." As a matter of fact, it is possible to achieve a relatively low score without a single "incorrect" answer because of evident weakness in the qualities being measured.

Occasionally, an examination may consist entirely of an oral test – either an individual or a group oral. In such cases, information is sought concerning the technical knowledges and abilities of the candidate, since there has been no written examination for this purpose. More commonly, however, an oral test is used to supplement a written examination.

Who conducts interviews?

The composition of oral boards varies among different jurisdictions. In nearly all, a representative of the personnel department serves as chairman. One of the members of the board may be a representative of the department in which the candidate would work. In some cases, "outside experts" are used, and, frequently, a businessman or some other representative of the general public is asked to serve. Labor and management or other special groups may be represented. The aim is to secure the services of experts in the appropriate field.

However the board is composed, it is a good idea (and not at all improper or unethical) to ascertain in advance of the interview who the members are and what groups they represent. When you are introduced to them, you will have some idea of their backgrounds and interests, and at least you will not stutter and stammer over their names.

What should be done before the interview?

While knowledge about the board members is useful and takes some of the surprise element out of the interview, there is other preparation which is more substantive. It *is* possible to prepare for an oral interview – in several ways:

1) Keep a copy of your application and review it carefully before the interview

This may be the only document before the oral board, and the starting point of the interview. Know what education and experience you have listed there, and the sequence and dates of all of it. Sometimes the board will ask you to review the highlights of your experience for them; you should not have to hem and haw doing it.

2) Study the class specification and the examination announcement

Usually, the oral board has one or both of these to guide them. The qualities, characteristics or knowledges required by the position sought are stated in these documents. They offer valuable clues as to the nature of the oral interview. For example, if the job involves supervisory responsibilities, the announcement will usually indicate that knowledge of modern supervisory methods and the qualifications of the candidate as a supervisor will be tested. If so, you can expect such questions, frequently in the form of a hypothetical situation which you are expected to solve. NEVER go into an oral without knowledge of the duties and responsibilities of the job you seek.

3) Think through each qualification required

Try to visualize the kind of questions you would ask if you were a board member. How well could you answer them? Try especially to appraise your own knowledge and background in each area, *measured against the job sought*, and identify any areas in which you are weak. Be critical and realistic – do not flatter yourself.

4) Do some general reading in areas in which you feel you may be weak

For example, if the job involves supervision and your past experience has NOT, some general reading in supervisory methods and practices, particularly in the field of human relations, might be useful. Do NOT study agency procedures or detailed manuals. The oral board will be testing your understanding and capacity, not your memory.

5) Get a good night's sleep and watch your general health and mental attitude

You will want a clear head at the interview. Take care of a cold or any other minor ailment, and of course, no hangovers.

What should be done on the day of the interview?

Now comes the day of the interview itself. Give yourself plenty of time to get there. Plan to arrive somewhat ahead of the scheduled time, particularly if your appointment is in the fore part of the day. If a previous candidate fails to appear, the board might be ready for you a bit early. By early afternoon an oral board is almost invariably behind schedule if there are many candidates, and you may have to wait. Take along a book or magazine to read, or your application to review, but leave any extraneous material in the waiting room when you go in for your interview. In any event, relax and compose yourself.

The matter of dress is important. The board is forming impressions about you – from your experience, your manners, your attitude, and your appearance. Give your personal appearance careful attention. Dress your best, but not your flashiest. Choose conservative, appropriate clothing, and be sure it is immaculate. This is a business interview, and your appearance should indicate that you regard it as such. Besides, being well groomed and properly dressed will help boost your confidence.

Sooner or later, someone will call your name and escort you into the interview room. *This is it.* From here on you are on your own. It is too late for any more preparation. But remember, you asked for this opportunity to prove your fitness, and you are here because your request was granted.

What happens when you go in?

The usual sequence of events will be as follows: The clerk (who is often the board stenographer) will introduce you to the chairman of the oral board, who will introduce you to the other members of the board. Acknowledge the introductions before you sit down. Do not be surprised if you find a microphone facing you or a stenotypist sitting by. Oral interviews are usually recorded in the event of an appeal or other review.

Usually the chairman of the board will open the interview by reviewing the highlights of your education and work experience from your application – primarily for the benefit of the other members of the board, as well as to get the material into the record. Do not interrupt or comment unless there is an error or significant misinterpretation; if that is the case, do not hesitate. But do not quibble about insignificant matters. Also, he will usually ask you some question about your education, experience or your present job – partly to get you to start talking and to establish the interviewing "rapport." He may start the actual questioning, or turn it over to one of the other members. Frequently, each member undertakes the questioning on a particular area, one in which he is perhaps most competent, so you can expect each member to participate in the examination. Because time is limited, you may also expect some rather abrupt switches in the direction the questioning takes, so do not be upset by it. Normally, a board member will not pursue a single line of questioning unless he discovers a particular strength or weakness.

After each member has participated, the chairman will usually ask whether any member has any further questions, then will ask you if you have anything you wish to add. Unless you are expecting this question, it may floor you. Worse, it may start you off on an extended, extemporaneous speech. The board is not usually seeking more information. The question is principally to offer you a last opportunity to present further qualifications or to indicate that you have nothing to add. So, if you feel that a significant qualification or characteristic has been overlooked, it is proper to point it out in a sentence or so. Do not compliment the board on the thoroughness of their examination – they have been sketchy, and you know it. If you wish, merely say, "No thank you, I have nothing further to add." This is a point where you can "talk yourself out" of a good impression or fail to present an important bit of information. Remember, *you close the interview yourself.*

The chairman will then say, "That is all, Mr. _____, thank you." Do not be startled; the interview is over, and quicker than you think. Thank him, gather your belongings and take your leave. Save your sigh of relief for the other side of the door.

How to put your best foot forward

Throughout this entire process, you may feel that the board individually and collectively is trying to pierce your defenses, seek out your hidden weaknesses and embarrass and confuse you. Actually, this is not true. They are obliged to make an appraisal of your qualifications for the job you are seeking, and they want to see you in your best light. Remember, they must interview all candidates and a non-cooperative candidate may become a failure in spite of their best efforts to bring out his qualifications. Here are 15 suggestions that will help you:

1) Be natural – Keep your attitude confident, not cocky

If you are not confident that you can do the job, do not expect the board to be. Do not apologize for your weaknesses, try to bring out your strong points. The board is interested in a positive, not negative, presentation. Cockiness will antagonize any board member and make him wonder if you are covering up a weakness by a false show of strength.

2) Get comfortable, but don't lounge or sprawl

Sit erectly but not stiffly. A careless posture may lead the board to conclude that you are careless in other things, or at least that you are not impressed by the importance of the occasion. Either conclusion is natural, even if incorrect. Do not fuss with your clothing, a pencil or an ashtray. Your hands may occasionally be useful to emphasize a point; do not let them become a point of distraction.

3) Do not wisecrack or make small talk

This is a serious situation, and your attitude should show that you consider it as such. Further, the time of the board is limited – they do not want to waste it, and neither should you.

4) Do not exaggerate your experience or abilities

In the first place, from information in the application or other interviews and sources, the board may know more about you than you think. Secondly, you probably will not get away with it. An experienced board is rather adept at spotting such a situation, so do not take the chance.

5) If you know a board member, do not make a point of it, yet do not hide it

Certainly you are not fooling him, and probably not the other members of the board. Do not try to take advantage of your acquaintanceship – it will probably do you little good.

6) Do not dominate the interview

Let the board do that. They will give you the clues – do not assume that you have to do all the talking. Realize that the board has a number of questions to ask you, and do not try to take up all the interview time by showing off your extensive knowledge of the answer to the first one.

7) Be attentive

You only have 20 minutes or so, and you should keep your attention at its sharpest throughout. When a member is addressing a problem or question to you, give him your undivided attention. Address your reply principally to him, but do not exclude the other board members.

8) Do not interrupt

A board member may be stating a problem for you to analyze. He will ask you a question when the time comes. Let him state the problem, and wait for the question.

9) Make sure you understand the question

Do not try to answer until you are sure what the question is. If it is not clear, restate it in your own words or ask the board member to clarify it for you. However, do not haggle about minor elements.

10) Reply promptly but not hastily

A common entry on oral board rating sheets is "candidate responded readily," or "candidate hesitated in replies." Respond as promptly and quickly as you can, but do not jump to a hasty, ill-considered answer.

11) Do not be peremptory in your answers

A brief answer is proper – but do not fire your answer back. That is a losing game from your point of view. The board member can probably ask questions much faster than you can answer them.

12) Do not try to create the answer you think the board member wants

He is interested in what kind of mind you have and how it works – not in playing games. Furthermore, he can usually spot this practice and will actually grade you down on it.

13) Do not switch sides in your reply merely to agree with a board member

Frequently, a member will take a contrary position merely to draw you out and to see if you are willing and able to defend your point of view. Do not start a debate, yet do not surrender a good position. If a position is worth taking, it is worth defending.

14) Do not be afraid to admit an error in judgment if you are shown to be wrong

The board knows that you are forced to reply without any opportunity for careful consideration. Your answer may be demonstrably wrong. If so, admit it and get on with the interview.

15) Do not dwell at length on your present job

The opening question may relate to your present assignment. Answer the question but do not go into an extended discussion. You are being examined for a *new* job, not your present one. As a matter of fact, try to phrase ALL your answers in terms of the job for which you are being examined.

Basis of Rating

Probably you will forget most of these "do's" and "don'ts" when you walk into the oral interview room. Even remembering them all will not ensure you a passing grade. Perhaps you did not have the qualifications in the first place. But remembering them will help you to put your best foot forward, without treading on the toes of the board members.

Rumor and popular opinion to the contrary notwithstanding, an oral board wants you to make the best appearance possible. They know you are under pressure – but they also want to see how you respond to it as a guide to what your reaction would be under the pressures of the job you seek. They will be influenced by the degree of poise you display, the personal traits you show and the manner in which you respond.

ABOUT THIS BOOK

This book contains tests divided into Examination Sections. Go through each test, answering every question in the margin. We have also attached a sample answer sheet at the back of the book that can be removed and used. At the end of each test look at the answer key and check your answers. On the ones you got wrong, look at the right answer choice and learn. Do not fill in the answers first. Do not memorize the questions and answers, but understand the answer and principles involved. On your test, the questions will likely be different from the samples. Questions are changed and new ones added. If you understand these past questions you should have success with any changes that arise. Tests may consist of several types of questions. We have additional books on each subject should more study be advisable or necessary for you. Finally, the more you study, the better prepared you will be. This book is intended to be the last thing you study before you walk into the examination room. Prior study of relevant texts is also recommended. NLC publishes some of these in our Fundamental Series. Knowledge and good sense are important factors in passing your exam. Good luck also helps. So now study this Passbook, absorb the material contained within and take that knowledge into the examination. Then do your best to pass that exam.

EXAMINATION SECTION

EXAMINATION SECTION
TEST 1

DIRECTIONS: Each question or incomplete statement is followed by several suggested answers or completions. Select the one that BEST answers the question or completes the statement. *PRINT THE LETTER OF THE CORRECT ANSWER IN THE SPACE AT THE RIGHT.*

1. As a general rule, which of the following areas on a campus would be most in need of protection by a physical barrier?
   Areas

   A. set aside for group activities
   B. smaller than 40 feet in diameter
   C. with roof access
   D. less than 18 feet above ground

2. For a campus officer to be armed, it is customary for him to complete a signed statement pledging himself to certain guidelines. Which of the following would typically be included in such a statement?
   I. The firearm will never be used as a club or similar weapon.
   II. Before shooting directly at a person, the officer will fire at least one warning shot.
   III. The firearm is only to be drawn when the officer's life, or the life of another, is threatened.
   IV. Shots directed at a perpetrator should be intended to disable, rather than kill.
   The CORRECT answer is:

   A. I, III
   B. I, III, IV
   C. III *only*
   D. II, III, IV

3. An arrest that is made after the security officer sees the offense committed is known as an arrest on

   A. reasonable suspicion of probable cause
   B. view
   C. detention
   D. complaint

4. The gate valve alarm of a sprinkler system has sounded. This means that the

   A. sprinkler system has been activated
   B. main water riser to the valve has been shut off
   C. storage water level has dropped below minimum requirements
   D. secondary water valve has been closed

5. A *dry* fire — from burning wood, paper, or textiles — is classified as Class

   A. A   B. B   C. C   D. D

6. The main DISADVANTAGE associated with the use of local alarms in security systems is that
    A. sometimes nobody is around to hear them
    B. they are dependent on electrical power
    C. they must be placed in multiple locations
    D. they don't deter criminals from breaking and entering

7. Each of the following is a symptom exhibited by *huffers* of vapors produced by glue, gasoline, paint, or other substances EXCEPT
    A. slurred speech
    B. violent behavior
    C. coughing
    D. increased appetite

8. Legally, a theft from the inside of a vehicle that has been locked and entered unlawfully is called
    A. robbery
    B. grand larceny
    C. burglary
    D. petty larceny

9. Security problems that may be caused by severe heat include
    A. increased likelihood of loss of power
    B. electrical overheating
    C. greater ability for people to hide stolen property
    D. increased likelihood of fires

10. Which of the following campus features does the most to necessitate a 24-hour radio dispatcher?
    A
    A. residential community
    B. contractual installation such as food service
    C. valuable collection
    D. high-rise building or buildings

11. If rounds clocks are used by an officer on patrol,
    A. the clock areas should be evenly spaced
    B. each clock must be punched on every round, regardless of the order
    C. the clock locations should never be changed
    D. they should be punched in exactly the same order each time

12. Because of the operating costs involved, a _____ alarm system is used primarily for government-owned facilities.
    A. remote
    B. central station
    C. local
    D. proprietary station

13. When assisting victims at the scene of an accident, an officer may
    I. give nonprescription medication
    II. restrain a person who is having a seizure
    III. treat a victim for shock
    IV. give the person fluids if the person is conscious
    The CORRECT answer is:
    A. I only
    B. II only
    C. III, IV
    D. IV only

14. When a(n) _____ is NOT generally an occasion on which a person, automobile, or premises may be legally searched.

    A. subject is being held for questioning
    B. warrant has been obtained
    C. emergency situation exists
    D. lawful arrest has been made

15. After a crime has been committed, a(n) _____ makes the most useful interview subject.

    A. witness   B. victim   C. suspect   D. informant

16. A _____ lock generally offers the LEAST amount of security.

    A. combination   B. pin tumbler
    C. disc tumbler   D. cipher

17. Evacuation guidelines for most campus buildings provide for an area warden, stair guard, and a group leader who is appointed from among the building's management personnel. Typically, a group leader will be responsible for controlling and directing about _____ people, depending on the floor size and layout.

    A. 5   B. 15   C. 25   D. 35

18. The campus has just received a bomb threat, and a search is underway. When searching individual rooms, an officer should begin

    A. at the door and move in a circular path
    B. at the corners and move inward
    C. with the furniture and then check the fixtures
    D. at the ceiling and move to the floor

19. The highest percentage of crime on school campuses typically occurs in

    A. classrooms and private offices
    B. residence hall or dorms
    C. parking lots
    D. commercial installations such as bookstores and food service

20. For most security applications, a report listing the holder of keys must be filed

    A. twice daily   B. daily
    C. twice weekly   D. weekly

21. The best driving speed for vehicle patrol services is generally between _____ miles per hour.

    A. 5-10   B. 15-20   C. 25-30   D. 35-40

22. Which of the following statements is generally FALSE?

    A. An officer should never approach a group of people without requesting backup, even if it is not needed.
    B. The officer should never draw a weapon as a tactic for discouraging violence.
    C. An officer should never confront hostile persons alone.
    D. When using a flashlight, the officer should hold it sheltered close to his body.

23. In general, security personnel may make an arrest if they
    I. observe a suspect taking property
    II. know a felony has been committed but did not see it happen
    III. know a misdemeanor has been committed but did not see it happen
    The CORRECT answer is:

    A. I only B. I, II C. I, III D. II, III

24. Which of the following may be a visible symptom of the abuse of opiates such as morphine, codeine, or heroin?

    A. Antisocial behavior
    B. Constricted eye functions
    C. Pale, sweaty skin
    D. Rapid speech

25. A security officer is the first to arrive at the scene of an accident that has caused injury. The victim has an open wound that is bleeding dark red, in a steady stream. After taking precautions against blood-borne disease, the officer should

    A. flush the wound with water
    B. apply a tourniquet
    C. apply antiseptic
    D. apply direct pressure to the wound

26. When approaching a subject for a weapons search, the officer should inform the subject that the search is to be conducted

    A. after the subject has been apprehended
    B. from behind, with one hand placed on the subject's shoulder
    C. from the patrol car, through a bullhorn or intercom
    D. from a safe distance of at least five feet

27. Which of the following elements should be included in a shift report?
    I. Detailed accounts of reported incidents
    II. Time and number of patrol rounds completed
    III. Information on condition of lighting
    IV. Weather conditions
    The CORRECT answer is:

    A. I only
    B. II, III, IV
    C. III, IV
    D. I, II

28. A(n) _____ internal alarm would probably be most effective in protecting a safe or vault.

    A. audio
    B. ultrasonic
    C. photoelectric
    D. capacitance

29. A call has come in from a passenger on a stranded elevator to the switchboard operator. After the operator receives the relevant information, security and maintenance personnel are contacted. Security personnel should report to the

    A. floor where the elevator is stranded
    B. maintenance personnel for direction
    C. bottom floor
    D. top floor

30. The post indicator alarm of a sprinkler system has sounded. This means the   30.____

    A. sprinkler system has been activated
    B. main water riser to the valve has been shut off
    C. storage water level has dropped below minimum requirements
    D. secondary water valve has been closed

31. The primary goal of a private security officer at the scene of a recent crime is   31.____

    A. containment   B. witness interviews
    C. suspect apprehension   D. evidence gathering

32. If a security officer encounters an accident victim who has gone into shock, the officer   32.____
    should do each of the following EXCEPT

    A. keep the victim warm
    B. raise the victim's head
    C. treat injuries
    D. loosen the victim's clothing

33. For a security officer, the foundation of good report writing is considered to be   33.____

    A. through patrolling   B. good interviewing
    C. field note taking   D. outlining skills

34. The fundamental difference between a crime called *malicious destruction of property* and   34.____
    one called *vandalism* is one of

    A. jurisdiction
    B. apparent motive
    C. the monetary amount of damage
    D. the type of property that was damaged

35. The most commonly used form of access control in setting such as college campuses is   35.____

    A. cipher locks   B. compartmentalization
    C. flood lighting   D. entry gate posts

36. The _____ should be allowed input into the decision to arm security personnel for spe-   36.____
    cific situations or events.
        I.   employers of security personnel
        II. public
        III. security agency
        IV. local law enforcement agency
    The CORRECT answer is:

    A. I, III   B. I, IV
    C. II, III, IV   D. II, IV

37. Which of the following activities generally offers the greatest degree of flexibility in the   37.____
    delivery of security services?

    A. Report writing   B. Vehicle patrol
    C. Access control   D. Foot patrol

38. Which of the following is NOT a security concern that is generally associated with flooding? 38.___

    A. Usefulness of parking areas
    B. Evacuation plans
    C. Bursting water pipes
    D. Looting

39. Which of the following is a use-of-force guideline for private security personnel? 39.___

    A. If equipment (such as a flashlight) is not designed for use as a weapon, it should never be used for that purpose.
    B. If necessary, use a weapon as a form of intimidation to forestall the necessity of having to use it.
    C. Saps or billyclubs should be displayed prominently on the officer's belt to discourage resistance.
    D. The officer should use whatever force is necessary to overcome perceived resistance.

40. An informant has come forward to offer information about a crime that has been committed on campus. The security officer believes it is important to understand the informant's motivation for coming forward. 40.___
    Generally, the officer should approach this subject

    A. at the beginning of the interview
    B. when the informant least expects it
    C. after the informant has given an account, but before the officer has asked any questions
    D. at the conclusion of the interview

KEY (CORRECT ANSWERS)

1.	D	11.	A	21.	B	31.	A
2.	A	12.	A	22.	D	32.	B
3.	B	13.	C	23.	B	33.	C
4.	D	14.	A	24.	B	34.	B
5.	A	15.	A	25.	D	35.	D
6.	A	16.	C	26.	D	36.	A
7.	D	17.	B	27.	B	37.	B
8.	C	18.	A	28.	D	38.	C
9.	D	19.	B	29.	A	39.	A
10.	A	20.	B	30.	B	40.	D

TEST 2

DIRECTIONS: Each question or incomplete statement is followed by several suggested answers or completions. Select the one that BEST answers the question or completes the statement. *PRINT THE LETTER OF THE CORRECT ANSWER IN THE SPACE AT THE RIGHT.*

1. The campus has just received a bomb threat, and a search is underway. When searching individual rooms, team members should be instructed to

    A. start the search in the center of the room and move outward from there
    B. search slowly, first searching the area from the floor to waist height
    C. place a marker on any suspicious looking item
    D. enter a room completely before beginning the search

2. When on a foot patrol assignment, an officer should

    A. turn the lights off whenever leaving a building
    B. stick to the shadows and avoid being seen
    C. observe the area to be patrolled before entering
    D. stick to the same pattern of patrolling

3. Chemical fires are classified as Class

    A. A   B. B   C. C   D. D

4. If campus security officers are to be armed, a _____ is typically most appropriate for their use.

    A. shotgun
    B. short-nosed .38-caliber revolver
    C. carbine
    D. long-nosed .357 magnum

5. Which of the following is NOT a guideline that should be followed by security personnel who are on foot patrol at night?

    A. Avoid being lit from the back
    B. View the area to be patrolled in advance, if possible
    C. When entering buildings and are moving from room to room, open doors as quietly as possible
    D. Keep the flashlight on thumb pressure only

6. Which of the following types of locks is most likely to be used with cabinets and desks?

    A. Combination lock   B. Disc tumbler lock
    C. Padlock   D. Cipher lock

7. When on patrol, security personnel have an obligation to report
    I. traffic patterns
    II. improper employee conduct
    III. observed hazards
    IV. poor housekeeping or maintenance practices

    The CORRECT answer is:

    A. I *only*   B. II, IV
    C. II, III, IV   D. III, IV

8. Towing policies for the enforcement of campus parking should include each of the following EXCEPT

   A. a contractual arrangement with a tow truck operator
   B. fines returnable to the local municipality, if possible
   C. the presence of a security officer at each towing incident
   D. a random pattern of towing that includes first-time offenders

9. Which of the following statements is generally TRUE?

   A. An officer should always display his badge prominently, especially when on night patrol.
   B. An officer should communicate with a dispatcher or other officers constantly while on duty.
   C. When approaching a vehicle, an officer should walk directly in front of the vehicle headlights.
   D. If a door has a window, an officer should look through it and examine the room before entering.

10. Which of the following is a sign that might be exhibited by a person who is on amphetamines or *uppers*?

    A. Loss of appetite
    B. Constricted pupils
    C. Rapid speech
    D. Uncontrolled laughing

11. Whenever possible, security policy guidelines for campus residence halls should include each of the following EXCEPT

    A. a periphery of high-intensity light around the exterior
    B. the use of interchangeable-core locking cylinders
    C. the use of only one main ground-floor entrance per building
    D. planting shrubs/trees outside first-floor rooms

12. An alarm system whose monitors are located in the main guard office is known as a _____ alarm system.

    A. remote
    B. central station
    C. local
    D. proprietary station

13. A security officer comes across a victim who has been badly burned. The officer should

    A. treat the victim for shock
    B. bandage the burn
    C. apply cold water to the burn
    D. apply an ointment or salve

14. Which of the following interview subjects typically presents a security officer with the least amount of difficulty?
    A(n)

    A. witness   B. victim   C. suspect   D. informant

15. Access control to any campus will be ineffective in any case if _____ are not provided.

    A. physical barriers
    B. weapons
    C. floodlights
    D. secure locks

16. Generally, security personnel may detain a person if
    I. it is known that the subject has information regarding a crime
    II. there is probable cause to believe the person has unlawfully taken property that can be recovered by holding the person for a reasonable period of time
    III. it is suspected that the person will commit a crime in the near future
    The CORRECT answer is:

    A. I, II B. II only C. III only D. I, III

17. In general, departmental record control should place a _____ day limit on the time allotted for the removal of files from the office by security personnel.

    A. 1 B. 2-3 C. 5-7 D. 10-15

18. Keys to gates, buildings, and other secured equipment must generally be issued and returned by officers

    A. every day
    B. every week
    C. every month
    D. annually

19. A crime has just been committed and a security officer is the first to arrive at the scene. Before the police arrive, a handful of campus officials arrive and request to enter the crime scene.
    The best way to handle this is to

    A. keep them out by any means necessary
    B. request their cooperation in remaining outside the scene until the police have arrived
    C. refer them to the security supervisor
    D. defer to their wishes

20. Which of the following phrases has a different meaning from the others?

    A. Incident report
    B. Post journal
    C. Shift report
    D. Post log

21. In order to be effective, combination locks used for access control should have AT LEAST _____ numbers.

    A. 3 B. 4 C. 5 D. 6

22. The simplest, most effective, and trouble-free peripheral alarm system for low-risk applications would probably involve

    A. magnetic switches
    B. button switches
    C. metallic foil tape
    D. audio switches

23. During a bomb search, a suspicious-looking package is found. Security personnel should

    A. move the package to a secure location
    B. place the package in water
    C. prevent anyone from touching the package
    D. place a tag on the package

24. When assisting a victim at the scene of an accident, an officer may
    I. describe an injury to the victim
    II. lift an injured person to a sitting position
    III. try to remove a foreign object from the victim's eye
    IV. attempt to keep the victim warm
    The CORRECT answer is:

    A. I only   B. II, III   C. IV only   D. III, IV

25. Each of the following is a symptom of shock EXCEPT

    A. slow pulse
    B. intense thirst
    C. dilated pupils
    D. irregular breathing

26. When on vehicle patrol, an officer should

    A. park directly in front of the building to be inspected
    B. observe from a distance or in a drive-by before driving into an area
    C. use spotlights to meet inspection requirements
    D. keep all windows closed while driving

27. Which of the following is a guideline to be followed by security personnel who are required to testify in court?

    A. Avoid asking attorneys to repeat their questions
    B. Never use the phrase *I think*
    C. Answer all questions as completely as possible
    D. Avoid looking directly at the judge or jury

28. Of the following types of arrest, the one that is most troublesome for security officers to justify is one that is made on

    A. reasonable suspicion of probable cause
    B. view
    C. detention
    D. complaint

29. The primary DISADVANTAGE associated with the use of central station alarm monitors is that

    A. time is lost from the time the signal is received until personnel arrive at the alarm area
    B. they do not provide a link to outside law enforcement agencies
    C. intruders are tipped off that the alarm has been activated
    D. they do not pin down the exact location of the alarm site

30. When writing any report, a security officer should

    A. write in the third person
    B. make sure there is at least one copy made
    C. use a formal outline
    D. use as few words as possible

31. Generally, campus property such as audio-visual equipment and office machinery should be inventoried at LEAST

   A. monthly
   B. quarterly
   C. annually
   D. every two years

32. Security personnel who carry firearms should generally be required to requalify themselves at a firing range every

   A. 4 months   B. 6 months   C. year   D. two years

33. Which of the following campus building areas is generally LEAST likely to be used for the placement of a bomb?

   A. Elevator shafts
   B. Toilets
   C. Roofs
   D. Electrical panels

34. If padlocks are used in security systems, it is recommended that they be made of

   A. aluminum
   B. case-hardened steel
   C. cast iron
   D. hardened steel

35. An officer should make certain assumptions about foot patrol assignments. Which of the following is NOT one of these?

   A. Some form of communication is available for the officer to obtain assistance or request instructions.
   B. Most foot patrol assignments are single-officer duties.
   C. Only buildings that are open for public access will be included in the assignment.
   D. Back-up officers are available but are at some distance.

36. Which of the following statements about security personnel arrests is/are generally TRUE?
   I. The subject does not have to be under control in order for there to be an arrest.
   II. Detaining a person is a technical arrest.
   III. An arrest is made with the arresting persons identifying themselves and make a statement such as *you are under arrest,* and either touch the suspect or the suspect agrees.
   IV. The authority for the arrest must be known by the suspect.
   The CORRECT answer is:

   A. I, II, IV
   B. II, III, IV
   C. III, IV
   D. I, III

37. As a general rule, an area that is less than _____ from another structure should be protected by a physical barrier.

   A. 14 feet   B. 25 feet   C. 64 feet   D. 100 yards

38. Security concerns associated with extreme cold include each of the following EXCEPT

   A. delayed communication
   B. physical danger from frozen surfaces
   C. increased opportunity for concealing objects under clothes
   D. integrity of plumbing systems

39. Fires from flammable liquids or grease are classified as Class 39.___

   A. A B. B C. C D. D

40. When interviewing the victim of a crime, which of the following is a guideline that should generally be followed by a security officer? 40.___

   A. Make sure at least one other officer is present.
   B. Maintain a calm, steady demeanor.
   C. Get the facts by any means necessary.
   D. Keep the victim away from others who are familiar to him/her.

KEY (CORRECT ANSWERS)

1. B	11. D	21. B	31. C
2. C	12. D	22. A	32. A
3. D	13. A	23. C	33. C
4. B	14. D	24. C	34. D
5. C	15. A	25. A	35. C
6. B	16. B	26. B	36. B
7. C	17. B	27. B	37. A
8. D	18. A	28. A	38. A
9. B	19. B	29. A	39. B
10. C	20. A	30. B	40. B

EXAMINATION SECTION
TEST 1

DIRECTIONS: Questions 1 through 5 are to be answered on the basis of the information, instructions, and sample question given below. Each question contains a GENERAL RULE, EXCEPTIONS, a PROBLEM, and the ACTION actually taken.

The GENERAL RULE explains what the special officer (security officer) should or should not do.

The EXCEPTIONS describe circumstances under which a special officer (security officer) should take action contrary to the GENERAL RULE.

However, an unusual emergency may justify taking an action that is not covered either by the GENERAL RULE or by the stated EXCEPTIONS.

The PROBLEM describes a situation requiring some action by the special officer (security officer).

ACTION describes what a special officer (security officer) actually did in that particular case.

Read carefully the GENERAL RULE and EXCEPTIONS, the PROBLEM, and the ACTION, and the mark A, B, C, or D in the space at the right in accordance with the following instructions:

   I. If an action is clearly justified under the general rule, mark your answer A.
   II. If an action is not justified under the general rule, but is justified under a stated exception, mark your answer B.
   III. If an action is not justified either by the general rule or by a stated exception, but does seem strongly justified by an unusual emergency situation, mark your answer C.
   IV. If an action does not seem justified for any of these reasons, mark your answer D.

SAMPLE QUESTION:

GENERAL RULE: A special officer (security officer) is not empowered to stop a person and search him for hidden weapons.
EXCEPTION: He may stop a person and search him if he has good reason to believe that he may be carrying a hidden weapon. Good reasons to believe he may be carrying a hidden weapon include (a) notification through official channels that a person may be armed, (b) a statement directly to the special officer (security officer) by the person himself that he is armed, and (c) the special officer's (security officer's) own direct observation.

PROBLEM: A special officer (security officer) on duty at a hospital clinic is notified by a woman patient at the clinic that a man sitting near her is making muttered threats that he has a gun and is going to shoot his doctor if the doctor gives him any trouble. Although the woman is upset, she seems to be telling the truth, and two other waiting patients con-

firm this. However, the special officer (security officer) approaches the man and sees no sign of a hidden weapon. The man tells the officer that he has no weapon.
ACTION: The special officer (security officer) takes the man aside into an empty office and proceeds to frisk him for a concealed weapon.

ANSWER: The answer cannot be A, because the general rule is that a special officer (security officer) is not empowered to search a person for hidden weapons. The answer cannot be B, because the notification did not come through official channels, the man did not tell the special officer (security officer) that he had a weapon, and the special officer (security officer) did not observe any weapon. However, since three people have confirmed that the man has said he has a weapon and is threatening to use it, this is pretty clearly an emergency situation that calls for action. Therefore, the answer is C.

1. GENERAL RULE: A special officer (security officer) on duty at a certain entrance is not to leave his post unguarded at any time.
   EXCEPTION: He may leave the post for a brief period if he first summons a replacement. He may also leave if it is necessary for him to take prompt emergency action to prevent injury to persons or property.
   PROBLEM: The special officer (security officer) sees a man running down a hall with a piece of iron pipe in his hand, chasing another man who is shouting for help. By going in immediate pursuit, there is a good chance that the special officer (security officer) can stop the man with the pipe.
   ACTION: The special officer (security officer) leaves his post unguarded and pursues the man.

   The CORRECT answer is:

   A. I   B. II   C. III   D. IV

2. GENERAL RULE: Special officers (security officers) assigned to a college campus are instructed not to arrest students for minor violations such as disorderly conduct; instead, the violation should be stopped and the incident should be reported to the college authorities, who will take disciplinary action.
   EXCEPTION: A special officer (security officer) may arrest a student or take other appropriate action if failure to do so is likely to result in personal injury or property damage, or disruption of school activities, or if the incident involves serious criminal behavior.
   PROBLEM: A special officer (security officer) is on duty in a college building where evening classes are being held. He is told that two students are causing a disturbance in a classroom. He arrives and finds that a fist fight is in progress and the classroom is in an uproar. The special officer (security officer) separates the two students who are fighting and takes them out of the room. Both of them seem to be intoxicated. They both have valid student ID cards.
   ACTION: The special officer (security officer) takes down their names and addresses for his report, then tells them to leave the building with a warning not to return this evening.

   The CORRECT answer is:

   A. I   B. II   C. III   D. IV

3. GENERAL RULE: A special officer (security officer) is not permitted to carry a gun while on duty.
   EXCEPTION: A special officer (security officer) who disarms a person must keep the weapon in his possession for the brief period before he can turn it over to the proper authorities. A special officer (security officer) who is NOT on duty may, like any other citizen, own and carry a gun if he has a proper permit from the Police Department.
   PROBLEM: A special officer (security officer) is assigned to a post where there have been a series of violent incidents in the past few days. He feels that these incidents could have been controlled much more easily if the people involved had seen that the special officer (security officer) had a gun. He has a gun at home, for which he has a valid permit.
   ACTION: The special officer (security officer) brings his gun when he goes on duty. He does not plan to use it, but just show people that he has it so that they will not start any trouble.

   The CORRECT answer is:

   A. I   B. II   C. III   D. IV

4. GENERAL RULE: No one except a licensed physician or someone acting directly under a physician's orders may legally administer medicine to another person.
   EXCEPTION: In a first aid situation, the special officer (security officer) is allowed to help a person suffering from a heart condition or other disease to take medicine which the person has in his possession, provided that the person is conscious and requests this assistance.
   PROBLEM: A special officer (security officer) on duty at a public building is told that a man has collapsed in the elevator. When the special officer (security officer) arrives at the scene, the man is barely conscious. He cannot speak, but he points to his pocket. The special officer (security officer) finds a pill bottle that says *one capsule in ease of need*. The man nods.
   ACTION: The special officer (security officer) puts one capsule in the man's hand and guides the man's hand to his mouth.

   The CORRECT answer is:

   A. I   B. II   C. III   D. IV

5. GENERAL RULE: In case of a fire drill or fire alarm, special officers (security officers) on patrol in a building are to remain in their assigned areas to assist in the evacuation of persons from the building and to make sure that no one takes advantage of the situation by stealing property that is left unguarded.
   EXCEPTION: Should there be an actual fire, special officers (security officers) will follow whatever instructions are given by the firefighters or police officers who arrive on the scene to take charge.
   PROBLEM: A special officer (security officer) is on duty patroling the fifth floor of a building when a fire alarm sounds. The fire is in a supply closet at one end of the fifth floor. All personnel have been evacuated from the floor. Neither police nor firemen have yet shown up.
   ACTION: The special officer (security officer) stays on the fifth floor at a safe distance from the supply closet.

   The CORRECT answer is:

   A. I   B. II   C. III   D. IV

KEY (CORRECT ANSWERS)

1. B
2. A
3. D
4. B
5. A

EXAMINATION SECTION
TEST 1

DIRECTIONS: Each question or incomplete statement is followed by several suggested answers or completions. Select the one that BEST answers the question or completes the statement. *PRINT THE LETTER OF THE CORRECT ANSWER IN THE SPACE AT THE RIGHT.*

1. The officer who investigates accidents is always required to make a complete and accurate report.
   Of the following, the BEST reason for this procedure is to

   A. protect the operating agency against possible false claims
   B. provide a file of incidents which can be used as basic material for an accident prevention campaign
   C. provide the management with concrete evidence of violations of the rules by employees
   D. indicate what repairs need to be made

2. It is suggested that an officer keep all persons away from the area of an accident until an investigation has been completed.
   This suggested procedure is

   A. *good;* witnesses will be more likely to agree on a single story
   B. *bad;* such action blocks traffic flow and causes congestion
   C. *good;* objects of possible use as evidence will be protected from damage or loss
   D. *bad;* the flow of normal pedestrian traffic provides an opportunity for an investigator to determine the cause of the accident

3. A man having business with your agency is arguing with you and accuses you of being prejudiced against him. Although you explain to him that this is not so, he demands to see your supervisor.
   Of the following, the BEST course of action for you to take is to

   A. continue arguing with him until you have worn him out or convinced him
   B. take him to your supervisor
   C. ignore him and walk away from him to another part of the office
   D. escort him out of the office

4. An officer receives instructions from his supervisor which he does not fully understand.
   For the officer to ask for a further explanation would be

   A. *good;* chiefly because his supervisor will be impressed with his interest in his work
   B. *poor;* chiefly because the time of the supervisor will be needlessly wasted
   C. *good;* chiefly because proper performance depends on full understanding of the work to be done
   D. *poor;* chiefly because officers should be able to think for themselves

5. A person is making a complaint to an officer which seems unreasonable and of little importance.
   Of the following, the BEST action for the officer to take is to

A. criticize the person making the complaint for taking up his valuable time
B. laugh over the matter to show that the complaint is minor and silly
C. tell the person that anyone responsible for his grievance will be prosecuted
D. listen to the person making the complaint and tell him that the matter will be investigated

6. A member of the department shall not indulge in intoxicating liquor while in uniform. A member of the department is not required to wear a uniform, and a uniformed member while out of uniform shall not indulge in intoxicants to an extent unfitting him for duty.
Of the following, the MOST correct interpretation of this rule is that a

   A. member, off duty, not in uniform, may drink intoxicating liquor
   B. member, not on duty, but in uniform, may drink intoxicating liquor
   C. member, on duty, in uniform, may drink intoxicants
   D. uniformed member, in civilian clothes, may not drink intoxicants

7. You have a suggestion for an important change which you believe will improve a certain procedure in your agency. Of the following, the next course of action for you to take is to

   A. try it out yourself
   B. submit the suggestion to your immediate supervisor
   C. write a letter to the head of your agency asking for his approval
   D. wait until you are asked for suggestions before submitting this one

8. An officer shall study maps and literature concerning his assigned area and the streets and points of interest nearby.
Of the following, the BEST reason for this rule is that

   A. the officer will be better able to give correct information to persons desiring it
   B. the officer will be better able to drive a vehicle in the area
   C. the officer will not lose interest in his work
   D. supervisors will not need to train the officers in this subject

9. In asking a witness to a crime to identify a suspect, it is a common practice to place the suspect with a group of persons and ask the witness to pick out the person in question.
Of the following, the BEST reason for this practice is that it will

   A. make the identification more reliable than if the witness were shown the suspect alone
   B. protect the witness against reprisals
   C. make sure that the witness is telling the truth
   D. help select other participants in the crime at the same time

10. It is most important for all officers to obey the "Rules and Regulations" of their agency.
Of the following, the BEST reason for this statement is that

    A. supervisors will not need to train their new officers
    B. officers will never have to use their own judgment
    C. uniform procedures will be followed
    D. officers will not need to ask their supervisors for assistance

Questions 11-13.

DIRECTIONS: Answer questions 11 to 13 SOLELY on the basis of the following paragraph.

All members of the police force must recognize that the people, through their representatives, hire and pay the police and that, as in any other employment, there must exist a proper employer-employee relationship. The police officer must understand that the essence of a correct police attitude is a willingness to serve, but at the same time, he should distinguish between service and servility, and between courtesy and softness. He must be firm but also courteous, avoiding even an appearance of rudeness. He should develop a position that is friendly and unbiased, pleasant and sympathetic, in his relations with the general public, but firm and impersonal on occasions calling for regulation and control. A police officer should understand that his primary purpose is to prevent violations, not to arrest people. He should recognize the line of demarcation between a police function and passing judgment which is a court function. On the other side, a public that cooperates with the police, that supports them in their efforts and that observes laws and regulations, may be said to have a desirable attitude.

11. In accordance with this paragraph, the PROPER attitude for a police officer to take is to

    A. be pleasant and sympathetic at all times
    B. be friendly, firm, and impartial
    C. be stern and severe in meting out justice to all
    D. avoid being rude, except in those cases where the public is uncooperative

12. Assume that an officer is assigned by his superior officer to a busy traffic intersection and is warned to be on the lookout for motorists who skip the light or who are speeding. According to this paragraph, it would be proper for the officer in this assignment to

    A. give a summons to every motorist whose ear was crossing when the light changed
    B. hide behind a truck and wait for drivers who violate traffic laws
    C. select at random motorists who seem to be impatient and lecture them sternly on traffic safety
    D. stand on post in order to deter violations and give offenders a summons or a warning as required

13. According to this paragraph, a police officer must realize that the primary purpose of police work is to

    A. provide proper police service in a courteous manner
    B. decide whether those who violate the law should be punished
    C. arrest those who violate laws
    D. establish a proper employer-employee relationship

Questions 14-15.

DIRECTIONS: Answer questions 14 and 15 SOLELY on the basis of the following paragraph.

If a motor vehicle fails to pass inspection, the owner will be given a rejection notice by the inspection station. Repairs must be made within ten days after this notice is issued. It is not necessary to have the required adjustment or repairs made at the station where the inspection occurred. The vehicle may be taken to any other garage. Re-inspection after repairs may be made at any official inspection station, not necessarily the same station which made the initial inspection. The registration of any motor vehicle for which an inspection sticker has not been obtained as required, or which is not repaired and inspected within ten days after inspection indicates defects, is subject to suspension. A vehicle cannot be used on public highways while its registration is under suspension.

14. According to the above paragraph, the owner of a car which does NOT pass inspection must

    A. have repairs made at the same station which rejected his car
    B. take the car to another station and have it re-inspected
    C. have repairs made anywhere and then have the car re-inspected
    D. not use the car on a public highway until the necessary repairs have been made

14.____

15. According to the above paragraph, the one of the following which may be cause for suspension of the registration of a vehicle is that

    A. an inspection sticker was issued before the rejection notice had been in force for ten days
    B. it was not re-inspected by the station that rejected it originally
    C. it was not re-inspected either by the station that rejected it originally or by the garage which made the repairs
    D. it has not had defective parts repaired within ten days after inspection

15.____

Questions 16-20.

DIRECTIONS: Answer questions 16 to 20 SOLELY on the basis of the following paragraph.

If we are to study crime in its widest social setting, we will find a variety of conduct which, although criminal in the legal sense, is not offensive to the moral conscience of a considerable number of persons. Traffic violations, for example, do not brand the offender as guilty of moral offense. In fact, the recipient of a traffic ticket is usually simply the subject of some good-natured joking by his friends. Although there may be indignation among certain groups of citizens against gambling and liquor law violations, these activities are often tolerated, if not openly supported, by the more numerous residents of the community. Indeed, certain social and service clubs regularly conduct gambling games and lotteries for the purpose of raising funds. Some communities regard violations involving the sale of liquor with little concern in order to profit from increased license fees and taxes paid by dealers. The thousand and one forms of political graft and corruption which infest our urban centers only occasionally arouse public condemnation and official action.

16. According to the paragraph, all types of illegal conduct are

    A. condemned by all elements of the community
    B. considered a moral offense, although some are tolerated by a few citizens
    C. violations of the law, but some are acceptable to certain elements of the community
    D. found in a social setting which is not punishable by law

16.____

17. According to the paragraph, traffic violations are generally considered by society as

    A. crimes requiring the maximum penalty set by the law
    B. more serious than violations of the liquor laws

17.____

C. offenses against the morals of the community
D. relatively minor offenses requiring minimum punishment

18. According to the paragraph, a lottery conducted for the purpose of raising funds for a church   18._____

    A. is considered a serious violation of law
    B. may be tolerated by a community which has laws against gambling
    C. may be conducted under special laws demanded by the more numerous residents of a community
    D. arouses indignation in most communities

19. On the basis of the paragraph, the MOST likely reaction in the community to a police raid on a gambling casino would be   19._____

    A. more an attitude of indifference than interest in the raid
    B. general approval of the raid
    C. condemnation of the raid by most people
    D. demand for further action since this raid is not sufficient to end gambling activities

20. The one of the following which BEST describes the central thought of this paragraph and would be MOST suitable as a title for it is   20._____

    A. CRIME AND THE POLICE
    B. PUBLIC CONDEMNATION OF GRAFT AND CORRUPTION
    C. GAMBLING IS NOT ALWAYS A VICIOUS BUSINESS
    D. PUBLIC ATTITUDE TOWARD LAW VIOLATIONS

Questions 21-23.

DIRECTIONS: Answer questions 21 to 23 SOLELY on the basis of the following paragraph.

The law enforcement agency is one of the most important agencies in the field of juvenile delinquency prevention. This is so not because of the social work connected with this problem, however, for this is not a police matter, but because the officers are usually the first to come in contact with the delinquent. The manner of arrest and detention makes a deep impression upon him and affects his life-long attitude toward society and the law. The juvenile court is perhaps the most important agency in this work. Contrary to the general opinion, however, it is not primarily concerned with putting children into correctional schools. The main purpose of the juvenile court is to save the child and to develop his emotional make-up in order that he can grow up to be a decent and well-balanced citizen. The system of probation is the means whereby the court seeks to accomplish these goals.

21. According to this paragraph, police work is an important part of a program to prevent juvenile delinquency because   21._____

    A. social work is no longer considered important in juvenile delinquency prevention
    B. police officers are the first to have contact with the delinquent
    C. police officers jail the offender in order to be able to change his attitude toward society and the law
    D. it is the first step in placing the delinquent in jail

22. According to this paragraph, the CHIEF purpose of the juvenile court is to   22._____

    A. punish the child for his offense
    B. select a suitable correctional school for the delinquent
    C. use available means to help the delinquent become a better person
    D. provide psychiatric care for the delinquent

23. According to this paragraph, the juvenile court directs the development of delinquents   23._____
    under its care CHIEFLY by

    A. placing the child under probation
    B. sending the child to a correctional school
    C. keeping the delinquent in prison
    D. returning the child to his home

Questions 24-27.

DIRECTIONS: Answer questions 24 to 27 SOLELY on the basis of the following paragraph.

When a vehicle has been disabled in the tunnel, the officer on patrol in this zone shall press the EMERGENCY TRUCK light button. In the fast lane, red lights will go on throughout the tunnel; in the slow lane, amber lights will go on throughout the tunnel. The yellow zone light will go on at each signal control station throughout the tunnel and will flash the number of the zone in which the stoppage has occurred. A red flashing pilot light will appear only at the signal control station at which the EMERGENCY TRUCK button was pressed. The emergency garage will receive an audible and visual signal indicating the signal control station at which the EMERGENCY TRUCK button was pressed. The garage officer shall acknowledge receipt of the signal by pressing the acknowledgment button. This will cause the pilot light at the operated signal control station in the tunnel to cease flashing and to remain steady. It is an answer to the officer at the operated signal control station that the emergency truck is responding to the call.

24. According to this paragraph, when the EMERGENCY TRUCK light button is pressed,   24._____

    A. amber lights will go on in every lane throughout the tunnel
    B. emergency signal lights will go on only in the lane in which the disabled vehicle happens to be
    C. red lights will go on in the fast lane throughout the tunnel
    D. pilot lights at all signal control stations will turn amber

25. According to this paragraph, the number of the zone in which the stoppage has occurred   25._____
    is flashed

    A. immediately after all the lights in the tunnel turn red
    B. by the yellow zone light at each signal control station
    C. by the emergency truck at the point of stoppage
    D. by the emergency garage

26. According to this paragraph, an officer near the disabled vehicle will know that the emer-   26._____
    gency tow truck is coming when

    A. the pilot light at the operated signal control station appears and flashes red
    B. an audible signal is heard in the tunnel

C. the zone light at the operated signal control station turns red
D. the pilot light at the operated signal control station becomes steady

27. Under the system described in the paragraph, it would be CORRECT to come to the conclusion that   27._____

    A. officers at all signal control stations are expected to acknowledge that they have received the stoppage signal
    B. officers at all signal control stations will know where the stoppage has occurred
    C. all traffic in both lanes of that side of the tunnel in which the stoppage has occurred must stop until the emergency truck has arrived
    D. there are two emergency garages, each able to respond to stoppages in traffic going in one particular direction

Questions 28-30.

DIRECTIONS: Answer questions 28 to 30 SOLELY on the basis of the following paragraphs.

In cases of accident, it is most important for an officer to obtain the name, age, residence, occupation, and a full description of the person injured, names and addresses of witnesses. He shall also obtain a statement of the attendant circumstances. He shall carefully note contributory conditions, if any, such as broken pavement, excavation, tights not burning, snow and ice on the roadway, etc. He shall enter all facts in his memorandum book and on Form 17 or Form 18 and promptly transmit the original of the form to his superior officer and the duplicate to headquarters.

An officer shall render reasonable assistance to sick or injured persons. If the circumstances appear to require the services of a physician, he shall summon a physician by telephoning the superior officer on duty and notifying him of the apparent nature of the illness or accident and the location where the physician will be required. He may summon other officers to assist if circumstances warrant.

In case of an accident or where a person is sick on city property, an officer shall obtain the information necessary to fill out card Form 18 and record this in his memorandum book and promptly telephone the facts to his superior officer. He shall deliver the original card at the expiration of his tour to his superior officer and transmit the duplicate to headquarters.

28. According to this quotation, the MOST important consideration in any report on a case of accident or injury is to   28._____

    A. obtain all the facts
    B. telephone his superior officer at once
    C. obtain a statement of the attendant circumstances
    D. determine ownership of the property on which the accident occurred

29. According to this quotation, in the case of an accident on city property, the officer should always   29._____

    A. summon a physician before filling out any forms or making any entries in his memorandum book
    B. give his superior officer on duty a prompt report by telephone

C. immediately bring the original of Form 18 to his superior officer on duty
D. call at least one other officer to the scene to witness conditions

30. If the procedures stated in this quotation were followed for all accidents in the city, an impartial survey of accidents occurring during any period of time in this city may be MOST easily made by

   A. asking a typical officer to show you his memorandum book
   B. having a superior officer investigate whether contributory conditions mentioned by witnesses actually exist
   C. checking all the records of all superior officers
   D. checking the duplicate card files at headquarters

Questions 31-55.

DIRECTIONS: In each of questions 31 to 55, select the lettered word or phrase which means MOST NEARLY the same as the first word in the row.

31. RENDEZVOUS

   A. parade   B. neighborhood
   C. meeting place D. wander about

32. EMINENT

   A. noted   B. rich   C. rounded   D. nearby

33. CAUSTIC

   A. cheap   B. sweet   C. evil   D. sharp

34. BARTER

   A. annoy   B. trade   C. argue   D. cheat

35. APTITUDE

   A. friendliness   B. talent
   C. conceit   D. generosity

36. PROTRUDE

   A. project   B. defend   C. choke   D. boast

37. FORTITUDE

   A. disposition   B. restlessness
   C. courage   D. poverty

38. PRELUDE

   A. introduction   B. meaning
   C. prayer   D. secret

39. SECLUSION

   A. primitive   B. influence
   C. imagination   D. privacy

40. RECTIFY
    A. correct   B. construct   C. divide   D. scold

41. TRAVERSE
    A. rotate   B. compose   C. train   D. cross

42. ALLEGE
    A. raise   B. convict   C. declare   D. chase

43. MENIAL
    A. pleasant   B. unselfish
    C. humble   D. stupid

44. DEPLETE
    A. exhaust   B. gather   C. repay   D. close

45. ERADICATE
    A. construct   B. advise   C. destroy   D. exclaim

46. CAPITULATE
    A. cover   B. surrender   C. receive   D. execute

47. RESTRAIN
    A. restore   B. drive   C. review   D. limit

48. AMALGAMATE
    A. join   B. force   C. correct   D. clash

49. DEJECTED
    A. beaten   B. speechless
    C. weak   D. low spirited

50. DETAIN
    A. hide   B. accuse   C. hold   D. mislead

KEY (CORRECT ANSWERS)

1. A	11. B	21. B	31. C	41. D
2. C	12. D	22. C	32. A	42. C
3. B	13. A	23. A	33. D	43. C
4. C	14. C	24. C	34. B	44. A
5. D	15. D	25. B	35. B	45. C
6. A	16. C	26. D	36. A	46. B
7. B	17. D	27. B	37. C	47. D
8. A	18. B	28. A	38. A	48. A
9. A	19. A	29. B	39. D	49. D
10. C	20. D	30. D	40. A	50. C

TEST 2

DIRECTIONS: Each question or incomplete statement is followed by several suggested answers or completions. Select the one that BEST answers the question or completes the statement. *PRINT THE LETTER OF THE CORRECT ANSWER IN THE SPACE AT THE RIGHT.*

1. AMPLE

    A. necessary   B. plentiful   C. protected   D. tasty

    1.____

2. EXPEDITE

    A. sue   B. omit   C. hasten   D. verify

    2.____

3. FRAGMENT

    A. simple tool   B. broken part
    C. basic outline   D. weakness

    3.____

4. ADVERSARY

    A. thief   B. partner   C. loser   D. foe

    4.____

5. ACHIEVE

    A. accomplish   B. begin   C. develop   D. urge

    5.____

Questions 6-10.

DIRECTIONS: Answer Questions 6 to 10 on the basis of the information given in the table on the following page. The numbers which have been omitted from the table can be calculated from the other numbers which are given.

NUMBER OF DWELLING UNITS CONSTRUCTED

Year	Private one-family houses	In private apt. houses	In public housing	Total dwelling units
1996	4,500	500	600	5,600
1997	9,200	5,300	2,800	17,300
1998	8,900	12,800	6,800	28,500
1999	12,100	15,500	7,100	34,700
2000	?	12,200	14,100	39,200
2001	10,200	26,000	8,600	44,800
2002	10,300	17,900	7,400	35,600
2003	11,800	18,900	7,700	38,400
2004	12,700	22,100	8,400	43,200
2005	13,300	24,300	8,100	45,700
TOTALS	105,900	?	?	?

6. According to this table, the average number of public housing units constructed yearly during the period 1996 through 2005 was

    A. 7,160   B. 6,180   C. 7,610   D. 6,810

    6.____

27

7. Of the following, the two years in which the number of private one-family homes constructed was GREATEST for the two years together is

   A. 1998 and 1999
   B. 1997 and 2003
   C. 1998 and 2004
   D. 2001 and 2002

8. For the entire period of 1996 through 2005, the total of all private one-family houses constructed exceeded the total of all public housing units constructed by

   A. 34,300
   B. 45,700
   C. 50,000
   D. 83,900

9. Of the total number of private apartment house dwelling units constructed in the ten years given in the table, the percentage which was constructed in 2002 was MOST NEARLY

   A. 5%
   B. 11%
   C. 16%
   D. 21%

10. Considering dwelling units of all types, the average number constructed annually in the period from 2001 through 2005 was GREATER than the average number constructed annually in the period from 1996 through 2000 by

    A. 16,480
    B. 33,320
    C. 79,300
    D. 82,400

11. A car speeds through the toll entrance of a 2 1/4 mile long bridge without paying the toll and reaches the other end of the bridge 1 minute and 30 seconds later. The car was traveling MOST NEARLY at a rate of _____ miles per hour.

    A. 60
    B. 70
    C. 80
    D. 90

12. During one week, 21,500 vehicles passed through the toll booths of a certain bridge. Of these, 550 were buses, 2,230 were trucks, and the rest were passenger cars. The toll charges were $3.50 for a passenger car, $7 for a truck and $14 for a bus. The total income for the week was

    A. $80,850
    B. $88,830
    C. $102,550
    D. $109,550

13. A bullet fired from a revolver travels 100 feet the first second, and each succeeding second it travels a distance 10% less than during the immediately preceding second. The number of feet the bullet will have traveled at the end of the fourth second is MOST NEARLY

    A. 272
    B. 320
    C. 344
    D. 360

14. An officer receives a uniform allowance of $500 a year in a lump sum. Of this amount, he spends $180 for a winter jacket and 40% of the remainder for two pairs of trousers. The officer now wishes to buy a winter overcoat which costs $240.
    The percentage of the purchase price of the overcoat by which he will be short is

    A. 20%
    B. 25%
    C. 48%
    D. 60%

15. It has been suggested that small light cars can be used for certain kinds of police work. These light vehicles can run 30 miles per gallon of gasoline as contrasted with standard cars which run only 15 miles per gallon. Assume gasoline costs the city $3.75 per gallon. During 9,000 miles of travel, use of the small light car in preference to the standard car would result in a saving in gasoline costs of MOST NEARLY

    A. $1,125
    B. $1,500
    C. $1,875
    D. $2,250

16. Out of a total of 34,750 felony complaints in 2006, 14,200 involved burglary. In 2005, there was a total of 32,300 felony complaints of which 12,800 were burglary.
Of the increase in felonies from 2005 to 2006, the increase in burglaries comprised APPROXIMATELY

   A. 27%   B. 37%   C. 47%   D. 57%

17. A certain city department has two offices which issue permits, one office handling twice as many applicants as the other. The smaller office grants permits to 40% of its applicants. The larger office handling twice as many applicants grants permits to 60% of its applicants.
If there were 900 applicants at both offices together on a given day, the total number of permits granted by both offices would be MOST NEARLY

   A. 420   B. 450   C. 480   D. 510

18. If a co-worker is not breathing after receiving an electric shock but is no longer in contact with the electricity, it is MOST important for you to

   A. avoid moving him
   B. wrap the victim in a blanket
   C. start artificial respiration promptly
   D. force him to take hot liquids

19. Employees using supplies from one of the first-aid kits available throughout the building are required to submit an immediate report of the occurrence.
Logical reasoning shows that the MOST important reason for this report is so that the

   A. supplies used will be sure to be replaced
   B. first-aid kit can be properly sealed again
   C. employee will be credited for his action
   D. record of first-aid supplies will be up-to-date

20. The BEST IMMEDIATE first-aid treatment for a scraped knee is to

   A. apply plain vaseline   B. wash it with soap and water
   C. apply heat   D. use a knee splint

21. Artificial respiration after a severe electrical shock is ALWAYS necessary when the shock results in

   A. unconsciousness   B. stoppage of breathing
   C. bleeding   D. a burn

22. The authority gives some of its maintenance employees instruction in first aid.
The MOST likely reason for doing this is to

   A. eliminate the need for calling a doctor in case of accident
   B. provide temporary emergency treatment in case of accident
   C. lower the cost of accidents to the authority
   D. reduce the number of accidents

23. The BEST IMMEDIATE first aid if a chemical solution splashes into the eyes is to

   A. protect the eyes from the light by bandaging
   B. rub the eyes dry with a towel

C. cause tears to flow by staring at a bright light
D. flush the eyes with large quantities of clean water

24. If you had to telephone for an ambulance because of an accident, the MOST important information for you to give the person who answered the telephone would be the

    A. exact time of the accident
    B. cause of the accident
    C. place where the ambulance is needed
    D. names and addresses of those injured

25. If a person has a deep puncture wound in his finger caused by a sharp nail, the BEST IMMEDIATE first aid procedure would be to

    A. encourage bleeding by exerting pressure around the injured area
    B. stop all bleeding
    C. prevent air from reaching the wound
    D. probe the wound for steel particles

26. In addition to cases of submersion, artificial respiration is a recommended first aid procedure for

    A. sunstroke   B. electrical shock   C. chemical poisoning   D. apoplexy

27. Assume that you are called on to render first aid to a man injured in an accident. You find he is bleeding profusely, is unconscious, and has a broken arm. There is a strong odor of alcohol about him.
    The FIRST thing for which you should treat him is the

    A. bleeding   B. unconsciousness   C. broken arm   D. alcoholism

28. In applying first aid for removal of a foreign body in the eye, an important precaution to be observed is NOT to

    A. attempt to wash out the foreign body
    B. bring the upper eyelid down over the lower
    C. rub the eye
    D. touch or attempt to remove a speck on the lower lid

29. The one of the following symptoms which is LEAST likely to indicate that a person involved in an accident requires first aid for shock is that

    A. he has fainted twice
    B. his face is red and flushed
    C. his skin is wet with sweat
    D. his pulse is rapid

30. When giving first aid to a person suffering from shock as a result of an auto accident, it is MOST important to

    A. massage him in order to aid blood circulation
    B. have him sip whiskey
    C. prop him up in a sitting position
    D. cover the person and keep him warm

Questions 31-34.

DIRECTIONS: Answer questions 31 to 34 SOLELY on the basis of the following paragraph.

Assume that you are an officer assigned to one large office which issues and receives applications for various permits and licenses. The office consists of one section where the necessary forms are issued; another section where fees are paid to a cashier; and desks where applicants are interviewed and their forms reviewed and completed. There is also a section containing tables and chairs where persons may sit and fill out their applications before being interviewed or paying the fees. your duties consist of answering simple questions, directing the public to the correct section of the office, and maintaining order.

31. A man who speaks English poorly asks you for assistance in obtaining and filling out an application for a permit. You should

    A. send him to an interviewer who can assist him
    B. try to determine what permit he wants and fill out the form for him
    C. refer the man to the office supervisor
    D. ask another applicant to help this person

31.____

32. The office becomes noisy and crowded, with people milling around waiting for service at the various sections.
    Of the following, the BEST action for you to take is to

    A. stand in a prominent place and in a loud voice request the people to be quiet
    B. direct all the people not being served to wait at the unoccupied tables until you call them
    C. line up the people in front of each section and keep the lines in good order
    D. tell the people to form a single line outside the office and let in a few at a time

32.____

33. A man who has just been denied a permit becomes angry and shouts that if he "knew the right people" he too could get a permit. His behavior is disturbing the office.
    Of the following, the BEST action for you to take is to

    A. order the man to leave at once since his business is done
    B. tell the man to be quiet and file another application
    C. suggest to the supervisor that a pamphlet be prepared explaining the requirements for permits in simple language
    D. ask an interviewer to explain the requirements for his permit to the person and his right of appeal

33.____

34. Just before the close of business, a man rushes in and insists on being interviewed for a permit because his present one expires that night.
    Of the following, the BEST action for you to take is to

    A. tell the man that the office is closed
    B. tell the man that there will be no penalty if he returns early the next morning
    C. inquire if an interviewer is still available to take care of him and send him to that desk
    D. tell the cashier to collect the fee and tell the man to return the next morning for an interview

34.____

35. Fingerprints are often taken of applicants for licenses. Of the following, the MOST valid reason for this procedure is that

   A. the license of someone who commits a crime can be more readily revoked
   B. applicants can be checked for possible criminal records
   C. it helps to make sure that the proper license fee is paid
   D. a complete employment record of the applicant is obtained

36. Assume that an officer is on patrol at 2 A.M. He notices that the night light inside one of the stores in a public building is out. The store is locked.
Of the following, the FIRST action for him to take at this time is to

   A. continue on his patrol since the light probably burned out
   B. enter the store by any means possible so he can check it
   C. report the matter to his superior
   D. shine his flashlight through the window to look for anything unusual

37. In questioning a man suspected of having committed a theft, the BEST procedure for an officer to follow is to

   A. induce the man to express his feelings about the police, the courts, and his home environment
   B. threaten him with beatings when he refuses to answer your questions
   C. make any promises necessary to get him to confess
   D. remain calm and objective

38. As an officer, you are on duty in one of the offices of a large public building. A woman who has just finished her business with this office comes to you and reports that her son who was with her is missing.
The one of the following which is the BEST action for you to take FIRST is to

   A. tell the mother that the child is probably all right and ask her to go to the local police station for help in finding the boy
   B. suggest that the mother wait in the office until the child turns up
   C. check nearby offices in an attempt to locate the child
   D. telephone the local police station and ask if any reports fitting the description of the child have been received

39. An officer assigned to patrol inside a public building at night has observed two men standing outside the doorway. Of the following, the MOST appropriate action for the officer to take FIRST is to

   A. approach the two men and ask them why they are standing there
   B. hide and wait for the two men to take some action
   C. phone the local police station and ask for help since these men may be planning criminal action
   D. check all the entrance doors of the building to make sure that they are locked

40. It is standard practice for special officers to inspect the restrooms in public buildings. This is done at regular intervals while on patrol.
Of the following, the BEST reason for this practice is to

   A. inspect sanitary conditions
   B. discourage loiterers and potential criminals

C. check the ventilation
D. determine if all the equipment and plumbing is working properly

41. While on duty in the evening as an officer assigned to a public building, you receive a report that a card game is going on in one of the offices. Gambling is forbidden on government property.
Of the following, the BEST course of action for you to take is to

    A. go to the office and order the card players to leave
    B. ignore the complaint since this is probably just harmless social card playing
    C. report the matter to the building manager the next day
    D. go to the office and, if warranted, issue an appropriate warning

42. It has been suggested that special officers establish good working relationships with the local police officers of the police department on duty in the neighborhood.
Of the following, the MOST valid reason for this practice is that

    A. a spirit of good feeling and high morale will be created among members of the police department
    B. local police officers will probably cooperate more readily with the special officer
    C. local police officers can take over the building patrol duties of the special officer in case he is absent
    D. special officers have an even stronger obligation than ordinary citizens to cooperate with the police

43. It has been proposed that an officer assigned to a public building at night remain at one location in the building, instead of walking on patrol through the building.
This proposal is

    A. *bad;* chiefly because the officer would probably sit instead of stand at the proper location
    B. *good;* chiefly because the officer could do a better job of watching the entire building from one point
    C. *bad;* chiefly because anyone seeking to enter the building for illegal purposes might be able to do so at a point other than where the special officer is on duty
    D. *good;* chiefly because his supervisors would know exactly where to find him

44. In a busy office, an officer has been assigned the duty of making sure that the public is served in the order of their arrival at the office and that some employee is always taking care of a person desiring help.
Of the following, the BEST method for the officer to follow is to

    A. line up the persons in the waiting room
    B. give a numbered ticket to each person waiting and call out the numbers, in order, when an employee becomes available
    C. loudly announce "next" when an employee is available to serve someone
    D. seat one person next to each employee's desk and let the others wait for the first vacant seat

45. Two men have broken into and entered a building at night. The officer on duty at this building sees them, chases them out, and then observes them in the adjoining building.
Of the following, the BEST course of action for the officer to take is to

    A. notify the local police station and be ready to aid the police
    B. enter the adjoining building to find the men
    C. notify the manager of his own building
    D. continue on duty since these men have left the building for which he is responsible

46. While an officer is on duty in a crowded waiting room, he finds a woman's purse on the floor.
Of the following, the FIRST course of action for him to take is to

    A. hold it up in the air, ask who owns it, and give it to whoever claims it
    B. keep the purse until someone claims it
    C. immediately deliver the purse to the "lost and found" desk
    D. ask the lady who is nearest to him if she lost a purse

47. Special officers often have the power of arrest.
Of the following, the BEST reason for this practice is to

    A. have the officer always arrest any person who refuses to obey his orders
    B. aid in maintaining order in places where he is assigned
    C. promote good public relations
    D. aid in preventing illegal use of public buildings by tenants or employees

48. An officer has told a mother that he found her son writing on the walls of the building with chalk. The mother tells the officer that he should be more concerned with "crooks" than with children's minor pranks.
Of the following, the BEST answer for the officer to make to this woman is that

    A. children should be taught good conduct by their parents
    B. damage to public property means higher taxes
    C. serious criminals often begin their careers with minor violations
    D. it is his duty to enforce all rules and regulations

49. A man asks you, a special officer, where to get a certain kind of license not issued in your office. You don't know where such licenses are issued.
Of the following, the BEST procedure for you to follow is to

    A. refer him to the manager of the office
    B. get the information if you can and give it to the man
    C. tell the man to inquire at any police station house
    D. tell the man that you just do not know

50. Special officers are not permitted to ask private citizens to buy tickets for dances or other such social functions, not even when such functions are operated by charitable organizations. Of the following, the BEST reason for this rule is that

    A. private citizens are under no obligation to buy any such tickets
    B. not all groups are allowed equal opportunity in the sale of their tickets
    C. private citizens might complain to officials
    D. private citizens might feel they would not get proper service unless they bought such tickets

KEY (CORRECT ANSWERS)

1. B	11. D	21. B	31. A	41. D
2. C	12. B	22. B	32. C	42. B
3. B	13. C	23. D	33. D	43. C
4. D	14. A	24. C	34. C	44. B
5. A	15. A	25. A	35. B	45. A
6. A	16. D	26. B	36. D	46. C
7. C	17. C	27. A	37. D	47. B
8. A	18. C	28. C	38. C	48. D
9. B	19. A	29. B	39. D	49. B
10. A	20. B	30. D	40. B	50. D

10 (#2)

SOLUTIONS TO ARITHMETIC PROBLEMS

11. $2\frac{1}{4}$ miles are completed in 1 1/2 minutes (1 minute and 30 seconds)

   $\therefore 2\frac{1}{4} \div 1\frac{1}{2}$ = rate per minute

   $= \frac{9}{4} \div 1\frac{1}{2}$

   $= \frac{9}{4} \div \frac{3}{2}$

   $= \frac{9}{4} \times \frac{2}{3}$

   $= \frac{3}{2}$ miles per minute

   $\therefore \frac{3}{2} \times 60$ (minutes in an hour) = rate per hour = 90 miles per hour

   (Ans. D)

12. 550 + 2230 = 2780; 21,500 - 2780 = 18,720 passengers

550 buses at $14.00	=	$ 7,700
2230 trucks at $7.00	=	15,610
18720 passengers at $3.50	=	65,520
		$88,830

   (Ans. B)

13. Given: speed = 100 feet the first second

100 - 10 (10% of 100)	=	90 feet - the second second
90 - 9 (10% of 90)	=	81 feet - the third second
81 - 8.1 (10% of 81)	=	72.9 feet - the fourth second
		343.9 (total at end of the fourth second)

   (Ans. C)

14. Given: 500 = uniform allowance

$500 -	180	= $320	(amount left after buying winter jacket)
$320 x	40%	= $128	(amount spent for two pairs of trousers)
$320 -	128	= $192	(amount now left)

   Since the winter overcoat costs $240, he is now short $48 ($240 - 192) or 20% of the purchase price of the overcoat. ($48/240 = \frac{1}{5} = 20\%$)

(Ans. A)

15. Light care: 9000(miles)÷30(miles per gallon)×3.75(per gallon)

    $= \dfrac{9000}{30} \times 3.75$

    $= 300 \times 3.75$

    $= \$1,125$ (total gasoline cost)

    Standard cars: 9000 (miles) ÷ 15 (miles per gallon) × 3.75

    $= \dfrac{9000}{15} \times 3.75$

    $= 600 \times 3.75$

    $= \$2,250$ (total gasoline cost)

    ∴ use of light car would result in a saving in gasoline costs of $1,125 ($2,250 - $1,125).

    (Ans. A)

16. 2006: 14,200   (burglary)
    2005: 12,800   (burglary)
           1,400   (increase in burglaries)

    2006: 34,750   (felony)
    2005: 32,300   (felony)
           2,450   (increase in felonies

    ∴ $1400 \div 2450 = \dfrac{1400}{2450} = .57$

    WORK

    ```
              .57
         ─────────
    2450)1400.0
         1225.0
         ──────
          175.00
          171.50
    ```

    (Ans. D)

17. Given: smaller office: grants permits to 40% of 1/3 of the total number of applicants (900)

    larger office: grants permits to 60% of 2/3 of the total number of applicants (900)

    Solving: smaller office: $.40 \times \dfrac{1}{3} \times 900 = 120$ permits

    larger office: $.60 \times \dfrac{2}{3} \times 900 = \underline{360}$ permits

    $\overline{480}$ permits (total)

    (Ans. C)

EXAMINATION SECTION
TEST 1

DIRECTIONS: Each question or incomplete statement is followed by several suggested answers or completions. Select the one that BEST answers the question or completes the statement. *PRINT THE LETTER OF THE CORRECT ANSWER IN THE SPACE AT THE RIGHT.*

1. Of the following, the MOST important single factor in any building security program is   1.____

    A. a fool-proof employee identification system
    B. an effective control of entrances and exits
    C. bright illumination of all outside areas
    D. clearly marking public and non-public areas

2. There is general agreement that the BEST criterion of what is a good physical security system in a large public building is   2.____

    A. the number of uniformed officers needed to patrol sensitive areas
    B. how successfully the system prevents rather than detects violations
    C. the number of persons caught in the act of committing criminal offenses
    D. how successfully the system succeeds in maintaining good public relations

3. Which one of the following statements most correctly expresses the CHIEF reason why women were originally made eligible for appointment to the position of officer?   3.____

    A. Certain tasks in security protection can be performed best by assigning women.
    B. More women than men are available to fill many vacancies in this position.
    C. The government wants more women in law enforcement because of their better attendance records.
    D. Women can no longer be barred from any government jobs because of sex.

4. The MOST BASIC purpose of patrol by officers is to   4.____

    A. eliminate as much as possible the opportunity for successful misconduct
    B. investigate criminal complaints and accident cases
    C. give prompt assistance to employees and citizens in distress or requesting their help
    D. take persons into custody who commit criminal offenses against persons and property

5. The highest quality of patrol service is MOST generally obtained by   5.____

    A. frequently changing the post assignments of each officer
    B. assigning officers to posts of equal size
    C. assigning problem officers to the least desirable posts
    D. assigning the same officers to the same posts

6. The one of the following requirements which is MOST essential to the successful performance of patrol duty by individual officers is their   6.____

    A. ability to communicate effectively with higher-level officers
    B. prompt signalling according to a prescribed schedule to insure post coverages at all times

39

C. knowledge of post conditions and post hazards
D. willingness to cover large areas during periods of critical manpower shortages

7. Officers on patrol are constantly warned to be on the alert for suspicious persons, actions, and circumstances.
   With this in mind, a senior officer should emphasize the need for them to

   A. be cautious and suspicious when dealing officially with any civilian regardless of the latter's overt actions or the circumstances surrounding his dealings with the police
   B. keep looking for the unusual persons, actions, and circumstances on their posts and pay less attention to the usual
   C. take aggressive police action immediately against any unusual person or condition detected on their posts, regardless of any other circumstances
   D. become thoroughly familiar with the usual on their posts so as to be better able to detect the unusual

8. Of primary importance in the safeguarding of property from theft is a good central lock and key issuance and control system.
   Which one of the following recommendations about maintaining such a control system would be LEAST acceptable?

   A. In selecting locks to be used for the various gates, building, and storage areas, consideration should be given to the amount of security desired.
   B. Master keys should have no markings that will identify them as such and the list of holders of these keys should be frequently reviewed to determine the continuing necessity for the individuals having them.
   C. Whenever keys for outside doors or gates or for other doors which permit access to important buildings and areas are misplaced, the locks should be immediately changed or replaced pending an investigation.
   D. Whenever an employee fails to return a borrowed key at the time specified, a prompt investigation should be made by the security force.

9. In a crowded building, a fire develops in the basement, and smoke enters the crowded rooms on the first floor. Of the following, the BEST action for an officer to take after an alarm is turned in is to

   A. call out a warning that the building is on fire and that everyone should evacuate because of the immediate danger
   B. call all of the officers together for an emergency meeting and discuss a plan of action
   C. immediately call for assistance from the local police station to help in evacuating the crowd
   D. tell everyone that there is a fire in the building next door and that they should move out onto the streets through available exits

10. Which of the following is in a key position to carry out successfully a safety program of an agency? The

    A. building engineer   B. bureau chiefs
    C. immediate supervisors   D. public relations director

11. It is GENERALLY considered that a daily roll call inspection, which checks to see that the officers and their equipment are in good order, is   11.____

    A. *desirable,* chiefly because it informs the superior officer what men will have to purchase new uniforms within a month
    B. *desirable,* chiefly because the public forms their impressions of the organization from the appearance of the officers
    C. *undesirable,* chiefly because this kind of daily inspection unnecessarily delays officers in getting to their assigned patrol posts
    D. *undesirable,* chiefly because roll call inspection usually misses individuals reporting to work late

12. A supervising officer in giving instructions to a group of officers on the principles of accident investigation remarked, "A conclusion that appears reasonable will often be changed by exploring a factor of apparently little importance".   12.____
    Which one of the following precautions does this statement emphasize as MOST important in any accident investigation?

    A. Every accident clue should be fully investigated.
    B. Accidents should not be too promptly investigated.
    C. Only specially trained officers should investigate accidents.
    D. Conclusions about accident causes are highly unreliable.

13. On a rainy day, a senior officer found that 9 of his 50 officers reported to work. What percentage of his officers was ABSENT?   13.____

    A. 18%   B. 80%   C. 82%   D. 90%

14. Officer A and Officer B work at the same post on the same days, but their hours are different. Officer A comes to work at 9:00 A.M. and leaves at 5:00 P.M., with a lunch period between 12:15 P.M. and 1:15 P.M. Officer B comes to work at 10:50 A.M. and works until 6:50 P.M., and he takes an hour for lunch between 3:00 P.M. and 4:00 P.M. What is the total amount of time between 9:00 A.M. and 6:50 P.M. that only ONE officer will be on duty?   14.____

    A. 4 hours
    B. 4 hours and 40 minutes
    C. 5 hours
    D. 5 hours and 40 minutes

15. An officer's log recorded the following attendance of 30 officers: 15.____

    Monday   20 present;   10 absent
    Tuesday   28 present;   2 absent
    Wednesday   30 present;   0 absent
    Thursday   21 present;   9 absent
    Friday   16 present;   14 absent
    Saturday   11 present;   19 absent
    Sunday   14 present;   16 absent

    On the average, how many men were present on the weekdays (Monday - Friday)?

    A. 21   B. 23   C. 25   D. 27

16. An angry woman is being questioned by an officer when she begins shouting abuses at him.
    The BEST of the following procedures for the officer to follow is to

    A. leave the room until she has cooled off
    B. politely ignore anything she says
    C. place her under arrest by handcuffing her to a fixed object
    D. warn her that he will have to use force to restrain her making remarks

17. Of the following, which is NOT a recommended practice for an officer placing a woman offender under arrest?

    A. Assume that the offender is an innocent and virtuous person and treat her accordingly.
    B. Protect himself from attack by the woman.
    C. Refrain from using excessive physical force on the offender.
    D. Make the public aware that he is not abusing the woman.

Questions 18-21.

DIRECTIONS: Questions 18 through 21 are to be answered SOLELY on the basis of the following passage.

Specific measures for prevention of pilferage will be based on careful analysis of the conditions at each agency. The most practical and effective method to control casual pilferage is the establishment of psychological deterrents.

One of the most common means of discouraging casual pilferage is to search individuals leaving the agency at unannounced times and places. These spot searches may occasionally detect attempts at theft but greater value is realized by bringing to the attention of individuals the fact that they may be apprehended if they do attempt the illegal removal of property.

An aggressive security education program is an effective means of convincing employees that they have much more to lose than they do to gain by engaging in acts of theft. It is important for all employees to realize that pilferage is morally wrong no matter how insignificant the value of the item which is taken. In establishing any deterrent to casual pilferage, security officers must not lose sight of the fact that most employees are honest and disapprove of thievery. Mutual respect between security personnel and other employees of the agency must be maintained if the facility is to be protected from other more dangerous forms of human hazards. Any security measure which infringes on the human rights or dignity of others will jeopardize, rather than enhance, the overall protection of the agency.

18. The $100,000 yearly inventory of an agency revealed that $50 worth of goods had been stolen; the only individuals with access to the stolen materials were the employees. Of the following measures, which would the author of the preceding paragraph MOST likely recommend to a security officer?

    A. Conduct an intensive investigation of all employees to find the culprit.
    B. Make a record of the theft, but take no investigative or disciplinary action against any employee.
    C. Place a tight security check on all future movements of personnel.
    D. Remove the remainder of the material to an area with much greater security.

19. What does the passage imply is the percentage of employees whom a security officer should expect to be honest?

    A. No employee can be expected to be honest all of the time
    B. Just 50%
    C. Less than 50%
    D. More than 50%

20. According to the passage, the security officer would use which of the following methods to minimize theft in buildings with many exits when his staff is very small?

    A. Conduct an inventory of all material and place a guard near that which is most likely to be pilfered.
    B. Inform employees of the consequences of legal prosecution for pilfering.
    C. Close off the unimportant exits and have all his men concentrate on a few exits.
    D. Place a guard at each exit and conduct a casual search of individuals leaving the premises.

21. Of the following, the title BEST suited for this passage is:

    A. Control Measures for Casual Pilfering
    B. Detecting the Potential Pilferer
    C. Financial losses Resulting from Pilfering
    D. The Use of Moral Persuasion in Physical Security

22. Of the following first aid procedures, which will cause the GREATEST harm in treating a fracture?

    A. Control hemorrhages by applying direct pressure
    B. Keep the broken portion from moving about
    C. Reset a protruding bone by pressing it back into place
    D. Treat the suffering person for shock

23. During a snowstorm, a man comes to you complaining of frostbitten hands. PROPER first aid treatment in this case is to

    A. place the hands under hot running water
    B. place the hands in lukewarm water
    C. call a hospital and wait for medical aid
    D. rub the hands in melting snow

24. While on duty, an officer sees a woman apparently in a state of shock. Of the following, which one is NOT a symptom of shock?

    A. Eyes lacking luster
    B. A cold, moist forehead
    C. A shallow, irregular breathing
    D. A strong, throbbing pulse

25. You notice a man entering your building who begins coughing violently, has shortness of breath, and complains of severe chest pains.
    These symptoms are GENERALLY indicative of

    A. a heart attack
    B. a stroke
    C. internal bleeding
    D. an epileptic seizure

26. When an officer is required to record the rolled fingerprint impressions of a prisoner on the standard fingerprint form, the technique recommended by the F.B.I. as MOST likely to result in obtaining clear impressions is to roll

   A. all fingers away from the center of the prisoner's body
   B. all fingers toward the center of the prisoner's body
   C. the thumbs away from and the other fingers toward the center of the prisoner's body
   D. the thumbs toward and the other fingers away from the center of the prisoner's body

27. The principle which underlies the operation and use of a lie detector machine is that

   A. a person who is not telling the truth will be able to give a consistent story
   B. a guilty mind will unconsciously associate ideas in a very indicative manner
   C. the presence of emotional stress in a person will result in certain abnormal physical reactions
   D. many individuals are not afraid to lie

Questions 28-32.

DIRECTIONS: Questions 28 through 32 are based SOLELY on the following diagram and the paragraph preceding this group of questions. The paragraph will be divided into two statements. Statement one (1) consists of information given to the senior officer by an agency director; *this information will detail the specific security objectives the senior officer has to meet.* Statement two (2) gives the resources available to the senior officer.

NOTE: The questions are correctly answered only when all of the agency's objectives have been met and when the officer has used all his resources efficiently (i.e., to their maximum effectiveness) in meeting these objectives. All X's in the diagram indicate possible locations of officers' posts. Each X has a corresponding number which is to be used when referring to that location.

DIAGRAM

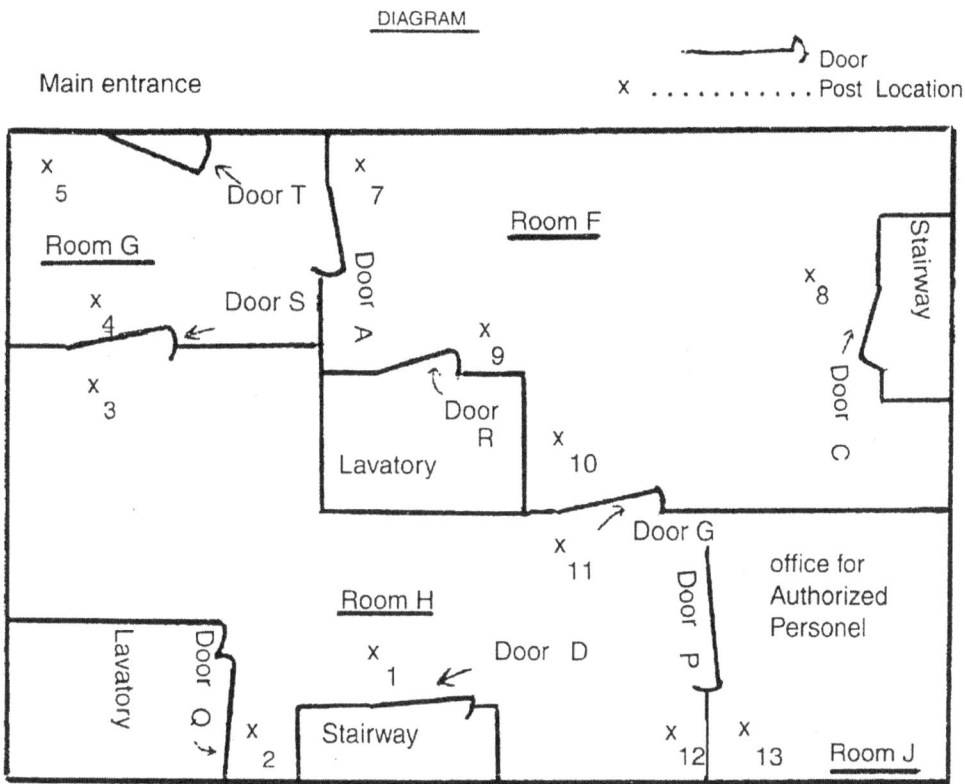

PARAGRAPH

PARAGRAPH

STATEMENT 1: Room G will be the public intake room from which persons will be directed to Room F or Room H; under no circumstances are they to enter the wrong room, and they are not to move from Room F to Room H or vice-versa. A minimum of two officers must be in each room frequented by the public at all times, and they are to keep unauthorized individuals from going to the second floor or into restricted areas. All usable entrances or exits must be covered.

STATEMENT 2: The senior officer can lock any door except the main entrance and stairway doors. He has a staff of five officers to carry out these operations.

NOTE: The senior officer is available for guard duty. Room J is an active office.

28. According to the instructions, how many officers should be assigned inside the office for authorized personnel (Room J)? 28._____

    A. 0   B. 1   C. 2   D. 3

29. In order to keep the public from moving between Room F and Room H, which door(s) can be locked without interfering with normal office operations? Door 29._____

    A. G   B. P   C. R and Q   D. S

30. When placing officers in Room H, the only way the senior officer can satisfy the agency's objectives and his manpower limitations is by placing men at locations   30.___

    A. 1 and 3   B. 1 and 12   C. 3 and 11   D. 11 and 12

31. In accordance with the instructions, the LEAST effective locations to place officers in Room F are locations   31.___

    A. 7 and 9   B. 7 and 10   C. 8 and 9   D. 9 and 10

32. In which room is it MOST difficult for each of the officers to see all the movements of the public? Room   32.___

    A. G   B. F   C. H   D. J

33. According to its own provisions, the Penal Law of the State has a number of general purposes.   33.___
    It would be LEAST accurate to state that one of these general purposes is to

    A. give fair warning of the nature of the conduct forbidden and the penalties authorized upon conviction
    B. define the act or omission and accompanying mental state which constitute each offense
    C. regulate the procedure which governs the arrest, trial and punishment of convicted offenders
    D. insure the public safety by preventing the commission of offenses through the deterrent influence of the sentences authorized upon conviction

34. Officers must be well-informed about the meaning of certain terms in connection with their enforcement duties. Which one of the following statements about such terms would be MOST accurate according to the Penal Law of the State? A(n)   34.___

    A. offense is always a crime
    B. offense is always a violation
    C. violation is never a crime
    D. felony is never an offense

35. According to the Penal Law of the State, the one of the following elements which must ALWAYS be present in order to justify the arrest of a person for criminal assault is   35.___

    A. the infliction of an actual physical injury
    B. an intent to cause an injury
    C. a threat to inflict a physical injury
    D. the use of some kind of weapon

36. A recent law of the State defines who are police officers and who are peace officers. The official title of this law is: The   36.___

    A. Criminal Code of Procedure
    B. Law of Criminal Procedure
    C. Criminal Procedure Law
    D. Code of Criminal Procedure

37. If you are required to appear in court to testify as the complainant in a criminal action, it would be MOST important for you to

    A. confine your answers to the questions asked when you are testifying
    B. help the prosecutor even if some exaggeration in your testimony may be necessary
    C. be as fair as possible to the defendant even if some details have to be omitted from your testimony
    D. avoid contradicting other witnesses testifying against the defendant

38. A senior officer is asked by the television news media to explain to the public what happened on his post during an important incident.
    When speaking with departmental permission in front of the tape recorders and cameras, the senior officer can give the MOST favorable impression of himself and his department by

    A. refusing to answer any questions but remaining calm in front of the cameras
    B. giving a detailed report of the wrong decisions made by his agency for handling the particular incident
    C. presenting the appropriate factual information in a competent way
    D. telling what should have been done during the incident and how such incidents will be handled in the future

39. Of the following suggested guidelines for officers, the one which is LEAST likely to be effective in promoting good manners and courtesy in their daily contacts with the public is:

    A. Treat inquiries by telephone in the same manner as those made in person
    B. Never look into the face of the person to whom you are speaking
    C. Never give misinformation in answer to any inquiry on a matter on which you are uncertain of the facts
    D. Show respect and consideration in both trivial and important contacts with the public

40. Assume you are an officer who has had a record of submitting late weekly reports and that you are given an order by your supervisor which is addressed to all line officers. The order states that weekly reports will be replaced by twice-weekly reports.
    The MOST logical conclusion for you to make, of the following, is:

    A. Fully detailed information was missing from your past reports
    B. Most officers have submitted late reports
    C. The supervisor needs more timely information
    D. The supervisor is attempting to punish you for your past late reports

41. A young man with long hair and "mod" clothing makes a complaint to an officer about the rudeness of another officer.
    If the senior officer is not on the premises, the officer receiving the complaint should

    A. consult with the officer who is being accused to see if the youth's story is true
    B. refer the young man to central headquarters
    C. record the complaint made against his fellow officer and ask the youth to wait until he can locate the senior officer
    D. search for the senior officer and bring him back to the site of the complainant

42. During a demonstration, which area should ALWAYS be kept clear of demonstrators? 42.___

    A. Water fountains   B. Seating areas
    C. Doorways   D. Restrooms

43. During demonstrations, an officer's MOST important duty is to 43.___

    A. aid the agency's employees to perform their duties
    B. promptly arrest those who might cause incidents
    C. promptly disperse the crowds of demonstrators
    D. keep the demonstrators from disrupting order

44. Of the following, what is the FIRST action a senior officer should take if a demonstration develops in his area without advance warning? 44.___

    A. Call for additional assistance from the police department
    B. Find the leaders of the demonstrators and discuss their demands
    C. See if the demonstrators intend to break the law
    D. Inform his superiors of the event taking place

45. If a senior officer is informed in the morning that a demonstration will take place during the afternoon at his assigned location, he should assemble his officers to discuss the nature and aspects of this demonstration. Of the following, the subject which it is LEAST important to discuss during this meeting is 45.___

    A. making a good impression if an officer is called before the television cameras for a personal interview
    B. the known facts and causes of the demonstration
    C. the attitude and expected behavior of the demonstrators
    D. the individual responsibilities of the officers during the demonstration

46. A male officer has probable reason to believe that a group of women occupying the ladies' toilet are using illicit drugs.
    The BEST action, of the following, for the officer to take is to 46.___

    A. call for assistance and, with the aid of such assistance, enter the toilet and escort the occupants outside
    B. ignore the situation but recommend that the ladies' toilet be closed temporarily
    C. immediately rush into the ladies' toilet and search the occupants therein
    D. knock on the door of the ladies' toilet and ask their permission to enter so that he will not be accused of trying to molest them

47. Assume that you know that a group of demonstrators will not cooperate with your request to throw handbills in a waste basket instead of on the sidewalk. You ask one of the leaders of the group, who agrees with you, to speak to the demonstrators and ask for their cooperation in this matter.
    Your request of the group leader is 47.___

    A. *desirable,* chiefly because an officer needs civilians to control the public since the officer is usually unfriendly to the views of public groups
    B. *undesirable,* chiefly because an officer should never request a civilian to perform his duties
    C. *desirable,* chiefly because the appeal of an acknowledged leader helps in gaining group cooperation

D. *undesirable,* chiefly because an institutional leader is motivated to maneuver a situation to gain his own personal advantage

48. A vague letter received from a female employee in the agency accuses an officer of improper conduct.
The initial investigative interview by the senior officer assigned to check the accusation should GENERALLY be with the

   A. accused officer
   B. female employee
   C. highest superior about disciplinary action against the officer
   D. immediate supervisor of the female employee

Questions 49-50.

DIRECTIONS: Questions 49 and 50 are to be answered SOLELY on the basis of the information in the following paragraph.

The personal conduct of each member of the Department is the primary factor in promoting desirable police-community relations. Tact, patience, and courtesy shall be strictly observed under all circumstances. A favorable public attitude toward the police must be earned; it is influenced by the personal conduct and attitude of each member of the force, by his personal integrity and courteous manner, by his respect for due process of law, by his devotion to the principles of justice, fairness, and impartiality.

49. According to the preceding paragraph, what is the BEST action an officer can take in dealing with people in a neighborhood?

   A. Assist neighborhood residents by doing favors for them.
   B. Give special attention to the community leaders in order to be able to control them effectively.
   C. Behave in an appropriate manner and give all community members the same just treatment.
   D. Prepare a plan detailing what he, the officer, wants to do for the community and submit it for approval.

50. As used in the paragraph, the word *impartiality* means *most nearly*

   A. observant   B. unbiased
   C. righteousness   D. honesty

KEY (CORRECT ANSWERS)

1. B	11. B	21. A	31. D	41. C
2. B	12. A	22. C	32. C	42. C
3. A	13. C	23. B	33. C	43. D
4. A	14. D	24. D	34. C	44. D
5. D	15. B	25. A	35. A	45. A
6. C	16. B	26. D	36. C	46. A
7. D	17. A	27. C	37. A	47. C
8. C	18. B	28. A	38. C	48. B
9. D	19. D	29. A	39. B	49. C
10. C	20. B	30. B	40. C	50. B

TEST 2

DIRECTIONS: Each question or incomplete statement is followed by several suggested answers or completions. Select the one that BEST answers the question or completes the statement. *PRINT THE LETTER OF THE CORRECT ANSWER IN THE SPACE AT THE RIGHT.*

Questions 1-5.

DIRECTIONS: Questions 1 through 5 consist of short paragraphs. Each paragraph contains one word which is INCORRECTLY used because it is NOT in keeping with the meaning of the paragraph. Find the word in each paragraph which is INCORRECTLY used, and then select as the answer the suggested word which should be substituted for the incorrectly used word.

SAMPLE QUESTION

In determining who is to do the work in your unit, you will have to decide just who does what from day to day. One of your lowest responsibilities is to assign work so that everybody gets a fair share and that everyone can do his part well.
    A. new   B. old   C. important   D. performance

EXPLANATION

The word which is NOT in keeping with the meaning of the paragraph is "lowest". This is the INCORRECTLY used word. The suggested word "important" would be in keeping with the meaning of the paragraph and should be substituted for "lowest". Therefore, the CORRECT answer is Choice C.

1. If really good practice in the elimination of preventable injuries is to be achieved and held in any establishment, top management must refuse full and definite responsibility and must apply a good share of its attention to the task. 1.____

    A. accept   B. avoidable   C. duties   D. problem

2. Recording the human face for identification is by no means the only service performed by the camera in the field of investigation. When the trial of any issue takes place, a word picture is sought to be distorted to the court of incidents, occurrences, or events which are in dispute. 2.____

    A. appeals   B. description
    C. portrayed   D. deranged

3. In the collection of physical evidence, it cannot be emphasized too strongly that a haphazard systematic search at the scene of the crime is vital. Nothing must be overlooked. Often the only leads in a case will come from the results of this search. 3.____

    A. important   B. investigation
    C. proof   D. thorough

4. If an investigator has reason to suspect that the witness is mentally stable or a habitual drunkard, he should leave no stone unturned in his investigation to determine if the witness was under the influence of liquor or drugs, or was mentally unbalanced either at the time of the occurrence to which he testified or at the time of the trial. 4.____

    A. accused   B. clue   C. deranged   D. question

5. The use of records is a valuable step in crime investigation and is the main reason every department should maintain accurate reports. Crimes are not committed through the use of departmental records alone but from the use of all records, of almost every type, wherever they may be found and whenever they give any incidental information regarding the criminal.

   A. accidental   B. necessary   C. reported   D. solved

Questions 6-8.

DIRECTIONS: Questions 6 through 8 are to be answered SOLELY on the basis of the following passage.

The mass media are an integral part of the daily life of virtually every American. Among these media, the youngest, television, is the most persuasive. Ninety-five percent of American homes have at least one television set, and on the average that set is in use for about 40 hours each week. The central place of television in American life makes this medium the focal point of a growing national concern over the effects of media portrayals of violence on the values, attitudes, and behavior of an ever increasing audience.

In our concern about violence and its causes, it is easy to make television a scapegoat. But we emphasise the fact that there is no simple answer to the problem of violence -- no single explanation of its causes, and no single prescription for its control. It should be remembered that America also experienced high levels of crime and violence in periods before the advent of television.

The problem of balance, taste, and artistic merit in entertaining programs on television are complex. We cannot countenance government censorship of television. Nor would we seek to impose arbitrary limitations on programming which might jeopardize television's ability to deal in dramatic presentations with controversial social issues. Nonetheless, we are deeply troubled by television's constant portrayal of violence, not in any genuine attempt to focus artistic expression on the human condition, but rather in pandering to a public preoccupation with violence that television itself has helped to generate.

6. According to the passage, television uses violence MAINLY

   A. to highlight the reality of everyday existence
   B. to satisfy the audience's hunger for destructive action
   C. to shape the values and attitudes of the public
   D. when it films documentaries concerning human conflict

7. Which one of the following statements is BEST supported by this passage?

   A. Early American history reveals a crime pattern which is not related to television.
   B. Programs should give presentations of social issues and never portray violent acts.
   C. Television has proven that entertainment programs can easily make the balance between taste and artistic merit a simple matter.
   D. Values and behavior should be regulated by governmental censorship.

8. Of the following, which word has the same meaning as countenance as it is used in the above passage?

   A. approve   B. exhibit   C. oppose   D. reject

Questions 9-12.

DIRECTIONS: Questions 9 through 12 are to be answered SOLELY on the basis of the following graph relating to the burglary rate in the city, 2003 to 2008, inclusive.

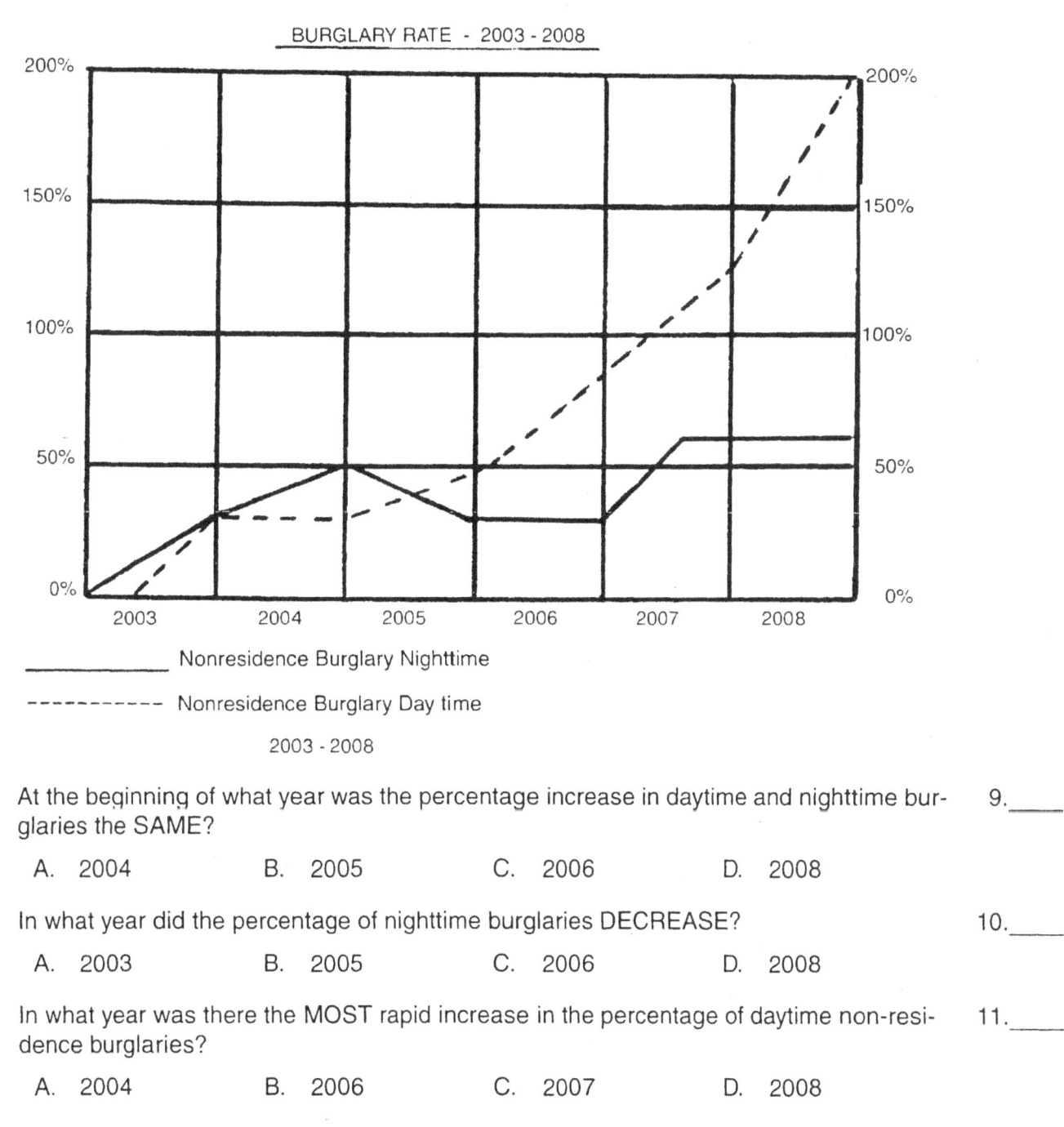

9. At the beginning of what year was the percentage increase in daytime and nighttime burglaries the SAME?

   A. 2004   B. 2005   C. 2006   D. 2008

10. In what year did the percentage of nighttime burglaries DECREASE?

    A. 2003   B. 2005   C. 2006   D. 2008

11. In what year was there the MOST rapid increase in the percentage of daytime non-residence burglaries?

    A. 2004   B. 2006   C. 2007   D. 2008

12. At the end of 2007, the actual number of nighttime burglaries committed

    A. was about 20%
    B. was 40%
    C. was 400
    D. cannot be determined from the information given

Questions 13-17.

DIRECTIONS: Questions 13 through 17 consist of two sentences numbered 1 and 2 taken from police officers' reports. Some of these sentences are correct according to ordinary formal English usage. Other sentences are incorrect because they contain errors in English usage or punctuation. Consider a sentence correct if it contains no errors in English usage or punctuation even if there may be other ways of writing the sentence correctly. Mark your answer to each question in the space at the right as follows:
   A. If only sentence 1 is correct, but not sentence 2
   B. If only sentence 2 is correct, but not sentence 1
   C. If sentences 1 and 2 are both correct
   D. If sentences 1 and 2 are both incorrect

SAMPLE QUESTION
   1. The woman claimed that the purse was her's.
   2. Everyone of the new officers was assigned to a patrol post.

EXPLANATION

Sentence 1 is INCORRECT because of an error in punctuation. The possessive words, "ours, yours, hers, theirs," do not have the apostrophe (').

Sentence 2 is CORRECT because the subject of the sentence is "Everyone" which is singular and requires the singular verb "was assigned".

Since only sentence 2 is correct, but not sentence 1, the CORRECT answer is B.

13. 1. Either the patrolman or his sergeant are always ready to help the public.
    2. The sergeant asked the patrolman when he would finish the report.

14. 1. The injured man could not hardly talk.
    2. Every officer had ought to hand in their reports on time.

15. 1. Approaching the victim of the assault, two large bruises were noticed by me.
    2. The prisoner was arrested for assault, resisting arrest, and use of a deadly weapon.

16. 1. A copy of the orders, which had been prepared by the captain, was given to each patrolman.
    2. It's always necessary to inform an arrested person of his constitutional rights before asking him any questions.

17. 1. To prevent further bleeding, I applied a tourniquet tothe wound.
    2. John Rano a senior officer was on duty at the time of the accident.

Questions 18-25.

DIRECTIONS: Answer each of Questions 18 through 25 SOLELY on the basis of the statement preceding the questions.

18. The criminal is one whose habits have been erroneously developed or, we should say, developed in anti-social patterns, and therefore the task of dealing with him is not one of punishment, but of treatment.
The basic principle expressed in this statement is BEST illustrated by the

   A. emphasis upon rehabilitation in penal institutions
   B. prevalence of capital punishment for murder
   C. practice of imposing heavy fines for minor violations
   D. legal provision for trial by jury in criminal cases

19. The writ of habeas corpus is one of the great guarantees of personal liberty. Of the following, the BEST justification for this statement is that the writ of habeas corpus is frequently used to

    A. compel the appearance in court of witnesses who are outside the state
    B. obtain the production of books and records at a criminal trial
    C. secure the release of a person improperly held in custody
    D. prevent the use of deception in obtaining testimony of reluctant witnesses

20. Fifteen persons suffered effects of carbon dioxide asphyxiation shortly before noon recently in a seventh-floor pressing shop. The accident occurred in a closed room where six steam presses were in operation. Four men and one woman were overcome.
    Of the following, the MOST probable reason for the fact that so many people were affected simultaneously is that

    A. women evidently show more resistance to the effects of carbon dioxide than men
    B. carbon dioxide is an odorless and colorless gas
    C. carbon dioxide is lighter than air
    D. carbon dioxide works more quickly at higher altitudes

21. Lay the patient on his stomach, one arm extended directly overhead, the other arm bent at the elbow, and with the face turned outward and resting on hand or forearm.
    To the officer who is skilled at administering first aid, these instructions should IMMEDIATELY suggest

    A. application of artificial respiration
    B. treatment for third degree burns of the arm
    C. setting a dislocated shoulder
    D. control of capillary bleeding in the stomach

22. The soda and acid fire extinguisher is the hand extinguisher most commonly used by officers. The main body of the cylinder is filled with a mixture of water and bicarbonate of soda. In a separate interior compartment, at the top, is a small bottle of sulphuric acid. When the extinguisher is inverted, the acid spills into the solution below and starts a chemical reaction. The carbon dioxide thereby generated forces the solution from the extinguisher.
    The officer who understands the operation of this fire extinguisher should know that it is LEAST likely to operate properly

    A. in basements or cellars
    B. in extremely cold weather
    C. when the reaction is of a chemical nature
    D. when the bicarbonate of soda is in solution

23. Suppose that, at a training lecture, you are told that many of the men in our penal institutions today are second and third offenders.
    Of the following, the MOST valid inference you can make SOLELY on the basis of this statement is that

    A. second offenders are not easily apprehended
    B. patterns of human behavior are not easily changed
    C. modern laws are not sufficiently flexible
    D. laws do not breed crimes

24. In all societies of our level of culture, acts are committed which arouse censure severe enough to take the form of punishment by the government. Such acts are crimes, not because of their inherent nature, but because of their ability to arouse resentment and to stimulate repressive measures.
Of the following, the MOST valid inference which can be drawn from this statement is that

   A. society unjustly punishes acts which are inherently criminal
   B. many acts are not crimes but are punished by society because such acts threaten the lives of innocent people
   C. only modern society has a level of culture
   D. societies sometimes disagree as to what acts are crimes

25. Crime cannot be measured directly. Its amount must be inferred from the frequency of some occurrence connected with it; for example, crimes brought to the attention of the police, persons arrested, prosecutions, convictions, and other dispositions, such as probation or commitment. Each of these may be used as an index of the amount of crime.
SOLELY on the basis of the foregoing statement, it is MOST correct to state that

   A. the incidence of crime cannot be estimated with any accuracy
   B. the number of commitments is usually greater than the number of probationary sentences
   C. the amount of crime is ordinarily directly correlated with the number of persons arrested
   D. a joint consideration of crimes brought to the attention of the police and the number of prosecutions undertaken gives little indication of the amount of crime in a locality

KEY (CORRECT ANSWERS)

1. B
2. A
3. D
4. C
5. D

6. B
7. A
8. A
9. A
10. B

11. D
12. D
13. D
14. D
15. B

16. C
17. A
18. A
19. C
20. B

21. A
22. B
23. B
24. D
25. C

SAMPLE QUESTIONS
BIOGRAPHICAL INVENTORY

The questions included in the Biographical Inventory ask for information about you and your background. These kinds of questions are often asked during an oral interview. For years, employers have been using interviews to relate personal history, preferences, and attitudes to job success. This Biographical Inventory attempts to do the same and includes questions which have been shown to be related to job success. It has been found that successful employees tend to select some answers more often than other answers, while less successful employees tend to select different answers. The questions in the Biographical Inventory do not have a single correct answer. Every choice is given some credit. More credit is given for answers selected more often by successful employees.

These Biographical Inventory questions are presented for illustrative purposes only. The answers have not been linked to the answers of successful employees; therefore, we cannot designate any "correct" answer(s).

DIRECTIONS: You may only mark ONE response to each question. It is possible that none of the answers applies well to you. However, one of the answers will surely be true (or less inaccurate) for you than others. In such a case, mark that answer. Answer each question honestly. The credit that is assigned to each response on the actual test is based upon how successful employees described themselves when honestly responding to the questions. *PRINT THE LETTER OF THE CORRECT ANSWER IN THE SPACE AT THE RIGHT.*

1. Generally, in your work assignments, would you prefer
   A. to work on one thing at a time
   B. to work on a couple of things at a time
   C. to work on many things at the same time

   1._____

2. In the course of a week, which of the following gives you the GREATEST satisfaction?
   A. Being told you have done a good job.
   B. Helping other people to solve their problems.
   C. Coming up with a new or unique way to handle a situation.
   D. Having free time to devote to personal interests.

   2._____

EXAMINATION SECTION
TEST 1

DIRECTIONS: Each question or incomplete statement is followed by several suggested answers or completions. Select the one that BEST answers the question or completes the statement. *PRINT THE LETTER OF THE CORRECT ANSWER IN THE SPACE AT THE RIGHT.*

1. The one of the following which is the BEST description of a properly objective investigator is one who

    A. is friendly and sensitive to the client's feelings, without becoming emotionally involved
    B. is distant and impersonal, remaining unaffected by what the client says
    C. lets personal emotions enter as far as the client's situation calls for them
    D. becomes emotionally involved with the client's situation but without showing this involvement

    1.____

2. The one of the following which is MOST necessary for successfully interviewing a person who belongs to a culture different from that of the investigator is for the investigator to

    A. have some appreciation of the other culture
    B. ignore those cultural differences which lead to bias
    C. stay away from sensitive, "touchy" issues
    D. assume the mannerisms of people in the other cultures

    2.____

3. In fact-finding interviews, it is generally assumed that the smaller the number of interviewees, the greater the increase of reliability with the addition of others. The PROPER number of interviewees needed to insure the accuracy of information obtained *generally* depends upon the

    A. educational level of those interviewed
    B. number of people who have the required information
    C. directness of the questions asked
    D. variability of the information received

    3.____

4. The one of the following which is generally MOST likely to be accurately described in an interview by an interviewee is

    A. the presence of a large painting in the investigator's office
    B. the number of people in the investigator's waiting room
    C. space relations
    D. duration of time

    4.____

5. The one of the following which is *generally* the BEST course of action for an investigator to take when interviewing a person who is reluctant to tell what he knows about a matter under investigation is to

    A. be curt and abrupt and threaten the person with the consequences of his withholding information
    B. be firm and severe and pressure the person into telling the needed information
    C. be patient and candid with the person being questioned about the investigation since doing otherwise is not ethical

    5.____

D. give the person false information about the investigation so he will give the needed information without realizing its importance

6. It is often recommended that an investigator prepare in advance a list of questions or topics to be covered in an interview. The MAIN reason for using such a check list is to

   A. allow investigations to be assigned to less efficient investigators
   B. eliminate a large amount of follow-up paper work
   C. aid the investigator in remembering to cover all important topics
   D. aid the investigator in maintaining an objective distance from the person interviewed

7. Usually, the CHIEF advantage of a directive approach in an interview is that

   A. the investigator maintains control over the course of the interview
   B. the person interviewed is more likely to be put at ease
   C. the person interviewed is generally left free to direct the interview
   D. the investigator will not suggest answers to the person interviewed

8. Usually, the CHIEF advantage of a non-directive approach by an investigator in conducting an interview is that

   A. the investigator generally conceals what he is looking for in the interview
   B. the person interviewed is more likely to express his true feelings about the topic under discussion
   C. the person interviewed is more likely to follow an idea introduced by the investigator
   D. the investigator can keep the discussion limited to topics he believes to be relevant

9. The one of the following which is generally the *least likely* to be accurate in a description of an event given to an investigator is a statement about

   A. the presence of an object
   B. the number of people, when their number is small
   C. locations of people
   D. duration of time

10. Assume that you, an investigator, are conducting a character investigation. In an interview, the one of the following character traits of the person being interviewed which can USUALLY be determined with a *good* degree of reliability is

    A. honesty B. dependability
    C. forcefulness D. perseverance

11. As an investigator, you have been assigned the task of obtaining a family's social history. The BEST place for you to interview members of the family while obtaining this social history would *generally* be in

    A. the family's home
    B. your agency's general offices
    C. the home of a friend of the family
    D. your own private office

3 (#1)

12. You, an investigator, are checking someone's work history. The way for you to get the MOST reliable information from a previous employer is to   12.____

    A. send personal letters; the employer will respond to the personal attention
    B. send form letters; the employer will cooperate readily since little time or effort is asked of him
    C. arrange a personal interview; the employer may offer information he would not care to put in a letter or speak over the phone
    D. telephone; this method is as effective as a personal interview and is much more convenient

13. The effect that attestation, or the formal taking of an oath, has on witness testimony is to   13.____

    A. decrease accuracy, since a witness under oath is more nervous about what is said
    B. make little difference, since the witness is not too swayed by an oath
    C. increase accuracy, since a witness under oath feels more responsibility for what is said
    D. eliminate inaccuracy unless there is deliberate perjury on the part of the witness

14. If an investigator obtains testimony from persons in interviews by means of interrogation or asking questions rather than by letting the person freely relate the testimony, what is said will GENERALLY be   14.____

    A. greater in range and less accurate
    B. greater in range and more accurate
    C. about the same in range and less accurate
    D. about the same in range and more accurate

15. Experienced investigators have learned to phrase their questions carefully in order to obtain the desired response. Of the following, the question which would *usually* elicit the MOST accurate answer is: 15.____

    A. "How old are you?"
    B. "What is your income?"
    C. "How are you today?"
    D. "What is the date of your birth?"

16. The one of the following questions which would *generally* lead to the LEAST reliable answer is   16.____

    A. "Did you see a wallet?"
    B. "Was the German Shepherd gray?"
    C. "Didn't you see the stop sign?"
    D. "Did you see the guard on duty?"

17. Some investigators may make a practice of observing details of the surroundings when interviewing in someone's home or office. Such a practice is *generally* considered   17.____

    A. *undesirable,* mainly because such snooping is an unwarranted, unethical invasion of privacy
    B. *undesirable,* mainly because useful information is rarely, if ever, gained this way
    C. *desirable,* mainly because, useful insights into the character of the person interviewed may be gained

63

D. *desirable,* mainly because it is impossible to evaluate a person adequately without such observation of his environment

18. The one of the following questions which will MOST often lead to a reliable answer is:

    A. "Was his hair very dark?"
    B. "Wasn't there a clock on the wall?"
    C. "Was the automobile white or gray?"
    D. "Did you see a motorcycle?"

19. The one of the following which can MOST accurately be determined by an investigator by means of interviewing is

    A. a persons's intelligence
    B. factual information about an event
    C. a person's aptitude for a specific task
    D. a person's perceptions of his own abilities

20. The one of the following which is *most likely* to help a person being interviewed feel at ease is for the investigator to

    A. let him start the conversation
    B. give him an abundance of time
    C. be relaxed himself
    D. open the interview by telling a joke

21. If the interviewee is to perceive some goal for himself in the interview and thus be motivated to participate in it, it is important that he clearly understand some of the aspects of the interview. Of the following aspects, the one the interviewee needs LEAST to understand is

    A. the purpose of the interview
    B. the mechanics of interviewing
    C. the use made of the information he contributes
    D. what will be expected of him in the interview

22. As an investigator working on a project requiring inter-agency cooperation, you find that employees of an agency involved in the project are constantly making it difficult for you to obtain necessary information. Of the following, the BEST action for you to take FIRST is to

    A. discuss the problem with your supervisor
    B. speak with your counterpart in the other agency
    C. discuss the problem with the head of the uncooperative agency
    D. contact the head of your agency

23. The investigator is justified in misleading the interviewee only when, in the investigator's judgment, this is clearly required by the problem being investigated. Such practice is

    A. *necessary;* there are times when complete honesty will impede a successful investigation
    B. *unnecessary ;* such a tactic is unethical and should never be employed
    C. *necessary;* an investigator must be guided by success rather than ethical considerations in an investigation

D. *unnecessary;* it is clearly doubtful whether such a practice will help the investigator conclude the investigation successfully

24. Assume that, in investigating a case of possible welfare fraud, it becomes necessary to hold an interview in the client's home in order to observe family interaction and conditions. Upon arriving, the investigator finds that the client's living room is noisy and crowded, with neighbors present and children running in and out. Of the following, the BEST course of action for the investigator to take is to 24.____

   A. conduct the interview in the living room after telling the children to behave, and asking the neighbors to leave
   B. tell the client that it is impossible to conduct the interview in the apartment, and make an appointment for the next day in the investigator's office
   C. suggest that they move from the living room into the kitchen where there is a table on which he can write
   D. try his best to conduct the interview in the noisy and crowded living room

25. You, an investigator, are giving testimony in court about a matter you have investigated. An attorney is questioning you in an abrasive, badgering way, and, in an insulting manner, calls into doubt your ability as an investigator. You lose your temper and respond angrily, telling the attorney to stop harassing and insulting you. Of the following, the BEST description of such a response is that it *is generally* 25.____

   A. *appropriate;* as a witness in court, you do not have to take insults from anybody, including an attorney
   B. *inappropriate; losing your* temper will show that you are weak and cannot be trusted as an investigator
   C. *appropriate;* a judge and jury will usually respect someone who responds strongly to unjust provocation
   D. *inappropriate;* such conduct is unprofessional and may unfavorably impress a judge and jury

KEY (CORRECT ANSWERS)

1.	A	11.	A
2.	A	12.	C
3.	D	13.	C
4.	A	14.	A
5.	C	15.	D
6.	C	16.	B
7.	A	17.	C
8.	B	18.	D
9.	D	19.	D
10.	C	20.	C

21. B
22. A
23. A
24. C
25. D

TEST 2

DIRECTIONS: Each question or incomplete statement is followed by several suggested answers or completions. Select the one that BEST answers the question or completes the statement. *PRINT THE LETTER OF THE CORRECT ANSWER IN THE SPACE AT THE RIGHT.*

1. The reliability of information obtained increases with the number of persons interviewed. The more the interviewees differ in their statements, the more persons it is necessary to interview to ascertain the true facts. According to this statement, the dependability of the information about an occurrence obtained from interviews is related to

    A. how many people are interviewed
    B. how soon after the occurrence an interview can be arranged
    C. the individual technique of the interviewer
    D. the interviewer's ability to detect differences in the statements of interviewees

2. An investigator interviews members of the public at his desk. The attitude of the public toward this department will probably be LEAST affected by this investigator's

    A. courtesy   B. efficiency
    C. height   D. neatness

3. The *one* of the following which is NOT effective in obtaining complete testimony from a witness during an interview is to

    A. ask questions in chronological order
    B. permit the witness to structure the interview
    C. make sure you fully understand the response to each question
    D. review questions to be asked beforehand

4. The person MOST likely to be a good interviewer is one who

    A. is able to outguess the person being interviewed
    B. tries to change the attitudes of the persons he interviews
    C. controls the interview by skillfully dominating the conversation
    D. is able to imagine himself in the position of the person being interviewed

5. When you are interviewing someone to obtain information, the BEST of the following reasons for you to repeat certain of his exact words is to

    A. *assure* him that appropriate action will be taken
    B. *encourage* him to elaborate on a point he has made
    C. *assure* him that you agree with his point of view
    D. *encourage* him to switch to another topic of discussion

6. You are interviewing a client who has just been assaulted. He has trouble collecting his thoughts and telling his story coherently. Which of the following represents the MOST effective method of questioning under these circumstances?

    A. Ask questions which structure the client's story chronologically into units, each with a beginning, middle and end.
    B. Ask several questions at a time to structure the interview.

67

C. Ask open-ended questions which allow the client to respond in a variety of ways.
D. Begin the interview with several detailed questions in order to focus the client's attention on the situation.

7. You are conducting an initial interview with a witness who expresses reluctance, even hostility, to being questioned. You feel it would be helpful to take some notes during the interview.
In this situation, it would be BEST to

   A. put off note-taking until a follow-up interview, and concentrate on establishing rapport with the witness
   B. explain the necessity of note-taking, and proceed to take notes during the interview
   C. make notes from memory after the witness has left
   D. take notes, but as unobtrusively as possible

8. You are interviewing the owner of a stolen car about facts relating to the robbery. After completing his statement, the car owner suddenly states that some of the details he has just related are not correct. You realize that this change might be significant.
Of the following, it would be BEST for you to

   A. ask the owner what other details he may have given incorrectly
   B. make a note of the discrepancy for discussion at a later date
   C. repeat your questioning on the details that were misstated until you have covered that area completely
   D. explain to the owner that because of his change of testimony, you will have to repeat the entire interview

9. Assume that you have been asked to get all the pertinent information from an employee who claims that she witnessed a robbery.
Which of the following questions is *least likely* to influence the witness's response?

   A. "Can you describe the robber's hair?"
   B. "Did the robber have a lot of hair?"
   C. "Was the robber's hair black or brown?"
   D. "Was the robber's hair very dark?"

10. In order to obtain an accurate statement from a person who has witnessed a crime, it is BEST to question the witness

    A. as soon as possible after the crime was committed
    B. after the witness has discussed the crime with other witnesses
    C. after the witness has had sufficient time to reflect on events and formulate a logical statement
    D. after the witness has been advised that he is obligated to tell the whole truth

11. Assume that your superior assigns you to interview an individual who, he warns, seems to be hightly "introverted." You should be aware that, during an interview, such a person is likely to

    A. hold views which are highly controversial in nature
    B. be domineering and try to control the direction of the interview
    C. resist answering personal questions regarding his background
    D. give information which is largely fabricated

12. A young woman was stabbed in the hand in her home by her estranged boyfriend. Her mother and two sisters were at home at the time.
Of the following, it would generally be BEST to interview the young woman in the presence of

    A. her mother *only*
    B. all members of her immediate family
    C. members of the family who actually observed the crime
    D. the official authorities

13. The one of the following statements concerning interviewing which is LEAST valid is that

    A. skill in interviewing can be improved by knowledge of the basic factors involving relations between people
    B. interviewing should become a routine and mechanical practice to the skilled and experienced interviewer
    C. genuine interest in people is essential for successful interviewing
    D. certain psychological traits characterize most people most of the time

14. The initial interview will normally be more of a problem to the interviewer than any subsequent interviews he may have with the same person because

    A. the interviewee is likely to be hostile
    B. there is too much to be accomplished in one session
    C. he has less information about the client than he will have later
    D. some information may be forgotten when later making record of this first interview

15. Continuous taking of notes during an interview is generally

    A. *desirable* because no important facts will be forgotten
    B. *undesirable* because it gives the person being interviewed a clue to the importance of the information being obtained from him
    C. *desirable* because the interviewer cannot write as fast as the person being interviewed can speak
    D. *undesirable* because it may put the person being interviewed ill at ease

16. "Carefully planned interviews tend to impose restrictions which leave little room for spontaneity." A flaw in this criticism of the planned interview is that it does NOT take into account that

    A. a planned interview obviates the need for spontaneity
    B. even the planned interview may be flexible
    C. not all planned interviews impose restrictions
    D. restrictions that result from planning are undesirable

17. Writing up the interview into a systematic report is BEST done

    A. in the presence of the subject, so that mistakes can be corrected immediately
    B. within a reasonably short time after the interview, so that nothing is forgotten
    C. no sooner than several days after the interview, so that the interviewer will have had plenty of time to think about it
    D. with the help of someone not present at the interview, so that an objective view can be obtained

18. While you are conducting an interview, the telephone on your desk rings. Of the following, it would be BEST for you to

   A. ask the interviewer at the next desk to answer your telephone and take the message for you
   B. excuse yourself, pick up the telephone, and tell the person on the other end you are busy and will call him back later
   C. ignore the ringing telephone and continue with the interview
   D. use another telephone to inform the operator not to put calls through to you while you are conducting an interview

19. An interviewee is at your desk, which is quite near to desks where other people work. He beckons you a little closer and starts to talk in a low voice as though he does not want anyone else to hear him. Under these circumstances, the BEST thing for you to do is to

   A. ask him to speak a little louder so that he can be heard
   B. cut the interview short and not get involved in his problems
   C. explain that people at other desks are not eavesdroppers
   D. listen carefully to what he says and give it consideration

20. Of the following, the BEST way for a person to develop competence as an interviewer is to

   A. attend lectures on interviewing techniques
   B. practice with employees on the job
   C. conduct interviews under the supervision of an experienced instructor
   D. attend a training course in counseling

21. During the course of an interview, it would be LEAST desirable for the investigator to

   A. correct immediately any grammatical errors made by an interviewee
   B. express himself in such a way as to be clearly understood
   C. restrict the interviewee to the subject of the interview
   D. make notes in a way that will not disturb the interviewee

22. Suppose that you are interviewing an eleven year old boy. The CHIEF point among the following for you to keep in mind is that a child, as compared with an adult, is generally

   A. more likely to attempt to conceal information
   B. a person of lower intelligence
   C. more garrulous
   D. more receptive to suggestive questions

23. In interviewing a person, "suggestive questions" should be avoided because, among the following,

   A. the answers to leading questions are not admissible in evidence
   B. an investigator must be fair and impartial
   C. the interrogation of a witness must be formulated according to his mentality
   D. they are less apt to lead to the truth

24. Among the following, it is generally desirable to interview a person outside his home or office because

A. the presence of relatives and friends may prevent him from speaking freely
B. a person's surroundings tend to color his testimony
C. the person will find less distraction outside his home or office
D. a person tends to dominate the interview when in familiar surroundings

25. For the interviewing process to be MOST successful, the interviewer should generally   25._____

    A. remind the person being interviewed that false statements will constitute perjury and will be prosecuted as such
    B. devise a single and unvarying pattern for all interviewing situations
    C. let the individual being interviewed control the content of the interview but not its length
    D. vary his interviewing approach as the situation requires it

KEY (CORRECT ANSWERS)

1.	A	11.	C
2.	C	12.	D
3.	B	13.	B
4.	D	14.	C
5.	B	15.	D
6.	A	16.	B
7.	B	17.	B
8.	C	18.	B
9.	A	19.	D
10.	A	20.	C

21. A
22. D
23. D
24. A
25. D

EXAMINATION SECTION
TEST 1

DIRECTIONS: Each question or incomplete statement is followed by several suggested answers or completions. Select the one that BEST answers the question or completes the statement. *PRINT THE LETTER OF THE CORRECT ANSWER IN THE SPACE AT THE RIGHT.*

1. Public organizations usually share each of the following customer-service problems with private organizations EXCEPT
   A. aversion to risk
   B. staff-heaviness
   C. provision of reverse incentives
   D. control-apportionment functions

   1.____

2. A service representative demonstrates interpersonal skills by
   A. identifying a customer's expectations
   B. learning how to use a new office telephone system
   C. studying a competitor's approach to service
   D. anticipating how a customer will react to certain situations

   2.____

3. Of the following, _____ is NOT generally considered to be a common reason for flaws in an organization's customer focus.
   A. commissioned employee compensation
   B. full problem-solving authority for front-line personnel
   C. inadequate hiring practices
   D. specific, case-oriented policy and procedural statements

   3.____

4. According to MOST research, approximately _____ of dissatisfied customers will actually complain or make their dissatisfaction with a product known to the organization.
   A. 5%   B. 25%   C. 50%   D. 75%

   4.____

5. Which of the following is an example of an expected benefit associated with a product or service?
   A. Before buying a car, a customer believes she will not have to take the car in for repairs every few months.
   B. A customer in a sporting goods store tells a salesperson exactly what kind of trolling motor will meet the requirements of the lakes the customer wanted to fish.
   C. A supermarket shopper buys a loaf of bread, believing that the bread will remain fresh for a few days.
   D. An airline passenger discover that the meals served on board are good.

   5.____

6. During a meeting with a service representative, a customer makes an apparently reasonable request. However, the representative knows that satisfying the customer's request will violate a rule that is part of the organization's policy. Although the representative feels that an exception to the rule should be made in this case, she is not sure whether an exception can or should be made.

   6.____

The BEST course of action for the representative would be to
A. deny the request and apologize, explaining the company policy
B. rely on good judgment and allow the request
C. try to steer the customer toward a similar but clearly permissible request
D. contact a manager or more experienced peer to handle the request

7. While organizing an effective customer service department, it would be LEAST effective to
    A. create procedures for relaying reasons for complaints to other departments
    B. set up a clear chain-of-command for handling specific customer complaints
    C. continually monitor performance of front-line personnel
    D. give front-line people full authority to resolve all customer dissatisfaction

8. Of the following, _____ is an example of *tangible* service.
    A. an interior decorator telling his/her ideas to a potential client
    B. a salesclerk giving a written cost estimate to a potential buyer
    C. an automobile salesman telling a showroom customer about a car's performance
    D. a stockbroker offering investment advice over the telephone

9. As a rule, a customer service representative who handles telephones should always answer a call within no more than _____ ring(s).
    A. 1   B. 3   C. 5   D. 8

10. In order to be as useful as possible to an organization, feedback received from customers should NOT be
    A. portrayed on a line graph or similar device
    B. used to provide a general overview
    C. focused on end-use customers
    D. available upon demand

11. Of all the customers who switch to competing organizations approximately _____ percent do so because of poor service.
    A. 25   B. 40   C. 75   D. 95

12. When customers offer information that is incorrect in their complaints, a service representative should do each of the following EXCEPT
    A. assume that the customer is making an innocent mistake
    B. look for opportunities to educate the customer
    C. calmly state a reasonable argument that will correct the customer's mistake
    D. believe the customer until he/she is able to find proof of his/her error

13. In order to insure that a customer feels comfortable in a face-to-face meeting, a service representative should
    A. avoid discussing controversial issues
    B. use personal terms such as *dear* or *friend*
    C. address the customer by his/her first name
    D. tell a few jokes

14. Customer satisfaction is MOST effectively measured in terms of
    A. cost   B. benefit   C. convenience   D. value

15. Making a sale is NOT considered good service when
    A. there are no alternatives to the subject of the customer's complaint
    B. when the original product or service is outdated
    C. an add-in feature will forestall other problems
    D. the product or service the customer has been using is the wrong product

16. When dealing with an indecisive customer, the service representative should
    A. expand available possibilities
    B. offer a way out of unsatisfying decisions
    C. ask probing questions for understanding
    D. steer the customer toward one particular decision

17. Of the following, _____ would NOT be a source of direct organizational service promises.
    A. advertising materials
    B. published organizational policies
    C. contracts
    D. the customer's past experience with the organization

18. Generally, the only kind of organization that can validly circumvent the requirements of customer service is one that
    A. cannot afford to staff an entire service department
    B. relies solely on the sale of ten or fewer items per year
    C. has little or no competition
    D. serves clients that are separated from consumers

19. When using the problem-solving approach to solve the problem of an upset customer, the service representative should FIRST
    A. express respect for the customer
    B. identify the customer's expectations
    C. outline a solution or alternatives
    D. listen to understand the problem

20. During face-to-face meetings with strangers such as service personnel, most North Americans consider a comfortable proximity to be
    A. 6 inches - 1 foot   B. 8 inches - 1½ feet
    C. 1½ - 2 feet   D. 2-4 feet

21. When answering phone calls, a service representative should ALWAYS do each of the following EXCEPT
    A. state his/her name
    B. give the name of the organization or department
    C. ask probing questions
    D. offer assistance

22. If a customer appears to be emotionally neutral when lodging a complaint, it would be MOST appropriate for a service representative to demonstrate _____ in reaction to the complaint.
    A. urgency   B. empathy   C. nonchalance   D. surprise

23. When soliciting customer feedback, standard practice is to limit the number of questions asked to APPROXIMATELY
    A. 3-5   B. 5-10   C. 10-20   D. 15-40

24. A customer has purchased an item from a company and has been told that the item will be delivered in two weeks. However, a customer service representative later discovers that deliveries are running about three days behind schedule.
    The MOST appropriate course of action for the representative would be to
    A. call the customer immediately, apologize for the delay, and await the customer's response
    B. call the customer a few days before delivery is due and explain that the delay is the fault of the delivery company
    C. immediately sent out a *loaner* of the ordered item to the customer
    D. wait for the customer to note the delay and contact the organization

25. Most research show that _____% of what is communicated between people during face-to-face meetings is conveyed through words alone.
    A. 10   B. 30   C. 50   D. 80

KEY (CORRECT ANSWERS)

1. D
2. D
3. B
4. A
5. B

6. D
7. B
8. B
9. B
10. B

11. B
12. C
13. A
14. D
15. A

16. B
17. D
18. C
19. A
20. C

21. C
22. D
23. B
24. A
25. A

TEST 2

DIRECTIONS: Each question or incomplete statement is followed by several suggested answers or completions. Select the one that BEST answers the question or completes the statement. *PRINT THE LETTER OF THE CORRECT ANSWER IN THE SPACE AT THE RIGHT.*

1. When working cooperatively to identify specific internal service targets, personnel typically encounter each of the following obstacles EXCEPT 1.____
   A. rapidly-changing work environment
   B. philosophical differences about the nature of service
   C. specialized knowledge of certain personnel exceeds that of others
   D. a chain-of-command that isolates the end user

2. Which of the following is an example of an external customer relationship? 2.____
   A. Baggage clerks to travelers
   B. Catering staff to flight attendants
   C. Managers to ticketing agents
   D. Maintenance workers to ground crew

3. When a service representative puts a customer's complaint in writing, results will be produced more quickly than if the representative had merely told someone. 3.____
   Which of the following is NOT generally considered to be a reason for this?
   A. The complaint can be more easily routed to parties capable of solving the problem.
   B. Management will understand the problem more clearly.
   C. The representative can more clearly see the main aspects of the complaint.
   D. The complaint and response will become a part of a public record.

4. A customer service representative creates a client file, which contains notes about what particular clients want, need, and expect. 4.____
   Which of the following basic areas of learning is the representative exercising?
   A. Interpersonal skills   B. Product and service knowledge
   C. Customer knowledge   D. Technical skills

5. A customer complains that a desired product, which is currently on sale, is needed in at least two weeks, but the company is out of stock and the product will not be available for another four weeks. 5.____
   Of the following, the BEST example of a service *recovery* on the part of a representative would be to
   A. apologize for the company's inability to serve the customer while expressing a wish to deal with the customer in the future
   B. attempt to steer the customer's interest toward an unrelated product
   C. offer a comparable model at the same sale price

78

6. Of the following, _____ is NOT generally considered to be a function of closed questioning when dealing with a customer.
   A. understanding requests
   B. getting the customer to agree
   C. clarifying what has been said
   D. summarizing a conversation

7. When dealing with a customer who speaks with a heavy foreign accent, a service representative should NOT
   A. speak loudly
   B. speak slowly
   C. avoid humor or witticism
   D. repeat what has been said

8. If a customer service representative is aware that time will be a factor in the delivery of service to a customer, the representative should FIRST
   A. warn the customer that the organization is under time constraints
   B. suggest that the customer return another time
   C. ask the customer to suggest a service deadline
   D. tell the customer when service can reasonably be expected

9. In relation to a customer service representative's view of an organization, the customer's view of the company tends to be
   A. more negative
   B. more objective
   C. broader in scope
   D. less forgiving

10. When asked to define the factors that determine whether they will do business with an organization, most customers maintain that _____ is the MOST important.
    A. friendly employees
    B. having their needs met
    C. convenience
    D. product pricing

11. While a customer is stating her service requirements, a service representative should do each of the following EXCEPT
    A. ask questions about complex or unclear information
    B. formulate a response to the customer's remarks
    C. repeat critical information
    D. attempt to roughly outline the customer's main points

12. If a customer service representative must deal with other member of a service team in order to resolve a problem, the representative should avoid
    A. conveying every single detail of a problem to others
    B. suggesting deadlines for problem resolution
    C. offering opinions about the source of the problem
    D. explaining the specifics concerning the need for resolution

13. Of the following, the LAST step in the resolution of a service problem should be
    A. the offer of an apology for the problem
    B. asking probing questions to understand and conform the nature of the problem
    C. listening to the customer's description of the problem
    D. determining and implementing a solution to the problem

14. _____ is a poor scheduling strategy for a customer service representative.
    A. Performing the easiest tasks first
    B. Varying work routines
    C. Setting deadlines that will allow some restful work periods
    D. Doing similar jobs at the same time

15. The MOST defensible reason for the avoidance of customer satisfaction guarantees is
    A. buyer remorse
    B. repeated customer contact
    C. high costs
    D. ability of buyers to take advantage of guarantees

16. A customer service representative demonstrates knowledge and courtesy to customers and is able to convey trust, competence, and confidence.
    Of the following service factors, the representative is demonstrating
    A. assurance
    B. responsiveness
    C. empathy
    D. reliability

17. If a service representative is involved in sales, _____ is NOT one of the primary pieces of information he/she will need to supply the customer.
    A. cost of product or service
    B. how the product works
    C. how to repair the product
    D. available payment plans

18. A customer appears to be experiencing extreme feelings of anger and frustration when loading a complaint.
    The MOST appropriate reaction for a service representative to demonstrate is
    A. urgency   B. empathy   C. nonchalance   D. surprise

19. Of the following obstacles to customer service, _____ is NOT generally considered to be unique to public organizations.
    A. ambivalence toward clients
    B. limited competition
    C. a rule-based mission
    D. clients who are not really customers

20. Most customers report that the MOST frustrating aspect of waiting in line for service is
    A. not knowing how long they will have to wait for service
    B. rudeness on the part of the service representatives
    C. being expected to wait for service at all
    D. unfair prioritizing on the part of service representatives

21. Which of the following is an example of an *assumed benefit* associated with a product or service?
    A customer
    A buys a sporty sedan and finds that its tight turning ratio makes it easy to park
    B. visits a fast-food restaurant because she is in a hurry to get dinner over with

C. buys a videotape and believes it will not cause damage to her VCR
D. tells a salesman that he wants to purchase a high-status automobile

22. On an average, for every complaint received by an organization, there are actually about _____ customers who have legitimate problems.
    A. 3   B. 5   C. 15   D. 25

23. Once a customer problem is identified, each of the following should become a part of the service recovery process EXCEPT
    A. apologizing
    B. an offer of compensation
    C. empathetic listening
    D. sympathy

24. As a rule, customers who telephone organizations should not be put on hold for any longer than
    A. 10 seconds
    B. 60 seconds
    C. 5 minutes
    D. 10 minutes

25. The LEAST effective way to make customers feel as if they are a part of a service team would be to ask them for
    A. information about similar products/services they have used
    B. opinions about how to solve problems
    C. personally contact the department that can best help them
    D. opinions about particular products and services

KEY (CORRECT ANSWERS)

1. B
2. A
3. D
4. C
5. D

6. A
7. A
8. C
9. C
10. B

11. B
12. C
13. A
14. A
15. B

16. A
17. C
18. B
19. B
20. A

21. C
22. D
23. D
24. B
25. C

READING COMPREHENSION
UNDERSTANDING AND INTERPRETING WRITTEN MATERIAL
EXAMINATION SECTION
TEST 1

DIRECTIONS: Each question or incomplete statement is followed by several suggested answers or completions. Select the one that BEST answers the question or completes the statement. *PRINT THE LETTER OF THE CORRECT ANSWER IN THE SPACE AT THE RIGHT.*

Questions 1-3.

DIRECTIONS: Questions 1 through 3 are to be answered SOLELY on the basis of the following passage.

When police officers search for a stolen car, they first check for the color of the car, then for make, model, year, body damage, and finally license number. The first five can be detected from almost any angle, while the recognition of the license number is often not immediately apparent. The serial number and motor number, though less likely to be changed than the easily substituted license number, cannot be observed in initial detection of the stolen car.

1. According to the above passage, the one of the following features which is LEAST readily observed in checking for a stolen car in moving traffic is
   A. license number
   B. serial number
   C. model
   D. make
   E. color

   1.____

2. The feature of a car that cannot be determined from most angles of observation is the
   A. make
   B. model
   C. year
   D. license number
   E. color

   2.____

3. Of the following, the feature of a stolen car that is MOST likely to be altered by a car thief shortly after the car is stolen is the
   A. license number
   B. motor number
   C. color
   D. model
   E. minor body damage

   3.____

Questions 4-5.

DIRECTIONS: Questions 4 and 5 are to be answered SOLELY on the basis of the following passage.

The racketeer is primarily concerned with business affairs, legitimate or otherwise, and preferably those which are close to the margin of legitimacy. He gets his best opportunities from business organizations which meet the need of large sections of the public for goods or services which are defined as illegitimate by the same public, such as prostitution, gambling, illicit drugs or liquor. In contrast to the thief, the racketeer and the establishments he controls deliver goods and services for money received.

4. From the above passage, it can be deduced that suppression of racketeers is difficult because
   A. victims of racketeers are not guilty of violating the law
   B. racketeers are generally engaged in fully legitimate enterprises
   C. many people want services which are not obtainable through legitimate sources
   D. the racketeers are well organized
   E. laws prohibiting gambling and prostitution are unenforceable

4._____

5. According to the above passage, racketeering, unlike theft, involves
   A. objects of value
   B. payment for goods received
   C. organized gangs
   D. public approval
   E. unlawful activities

5._____

Questions 6-8.

DIRECTIONS: Questions 6 through 8 are to be answered SOLELY on the basis of the following passage.

A number of crimes, such as robbery, assault, rape, certain forms of theft and burglary, are high visibility crimes in that it is apparent to all concerned that they are criminal acts prior to or at the time they are committed. In contrast to these, check forgeries, especially those committed by first offenders, have low visibility. There is little in the criminal act or in the interaction between the check passer and the person cashing the check to identify it as a crime. Closely related to this special quality of the forgery crime is the fact that, while it is formally defined and treated as a felonious or infamous crime, it is formally held by the legally untrained public to be a relatively harmless form of crime.

6. According to the above passage, crimes of *high visibility*
   A. are immediately recognized as crimes by the victim
   B. take place in public view
   C. always involve violence or the threat of violence
   D. usually are committed after dark
   E. can be observed from a distance

6._____

7. According to the above passage,
   A. the public regards check forgery as a minor crime
   B. the law regards check forgery as a minor crime
   C. the law distinguishes between check forgery and other forgery
   D. it is easier to spot inexperienced check forgers than other criminals
   E. it is more difficult to identify check forgers than other criminals

7._____

8. As used in the above passage, an *infamous* crime is
   A. a crime attracting great attention from the public
   B. more serious than a felony
   C. less serious than a felony
   D. more or less than a felony depending upon the surrounding circumstances
   E. the same as a felony

8._____

Questions 9-11.

DIRECTIONS: Questions 9 through 11 are to be answered SOLELY on the basis of the following passage.

Criminal science is largely the science of identification. Progress in this field has been marked and sometimes very spectacular because new techniques, instruments, and facts flow continuously from the scientists. But the crime laboratories are undermanned, trade secrets still prevail, and inaccurate conclusions are often the results. However, modern gadgets cannot substitute for the skilled intelligent investigator; he must be their master.

9. According to the above passage, criminal science 9.____
   A. excludes the field of investigation
   B. is primarily interested in establishing identity
   C. is based on the equipment used in crime laboratories
   D. uses techniques different from those used in other sciences
   E. is essentially secret in nature

10. Advances in criminal science have been, according to the above passage, 10.____
    A. extremely limited   B. slow but steady
    C. unusually reliable   D. outstanding
    E. infrequently worthwhile

11. A problem that has NOT been overcome completely in crime work is, according 11.____
    to the above passage,
    A. unskilled investigators
    B. the expense of new equipment and techniques
    C. an insufficient number of personnel in crime laboratories
    D. inaccurate equipment used in laboratories
    E. conclusions of the public about the value of this field

Questions 12-14.

DIRECTIONS: Questions 12 through 14 are to be answered SOLELY on the basis of the following passage.

The New York City Police Department will accept for investigation no report of a person missing from his residence, if such residence is located outside of New York City. The person reporting same will be advised to report such fact to the police department of the locality where the missing person lives, which will, if necessary, communicate officially with the New York City Police Department. However, a report will be accepted of a person who is missing from a temporary residence in New York City, but the person making the report will be instructed to make a report also to the police department of the locality where the missing person lives.

12. According to the above passage, a report to the New York City Police Depart- 12.____
    ment of a missing person whose permanent residence is outside of New York
    City will
    A. always be investigated provided that a report is also made to his local
       police authorities

B. never be investigated unless requested officially by his local police authorities
C. be investigated in cases of temporary New York City residence, but a report should always be made to his local police authorities
D. be investigated if the person making the report is a New York City resident
E. always be investigated and a report will be made to the local police authorities by the New York City Police Department

13. Of the following, the MOST likely reason for the procedure described in the above passage is that 13.____
    A. non-residents are not entitled to free police service from New York City
    B. local police authorities would resent interference in their jurisdiction
    C. local police authorities sometimes try to unload their problems on the New York City Police
    D. local police authorities may be better able to conduct an investigation
    E. few persons are erroneously reported as missing

14. Mr. Smith, who lives in Jersey City, and Mr. Jones, who lives in Newark, arrange to meet in New York City, but Mr. Jones doesn't keep the appointment. Mr. Smith telephones Mr. Jones several times the next day and gets no answer. Mr. Smith believes that something has happened to Mr. Jones. According to the above passage, Mr. Smith should apply to the police authorities of 14.____
    A. Jersey City
    B. Newark
    C. Newark and New York City
    D. Jersey City and New York City
    E. Newark, Jersey City, and New York City

Questions 15-17.

DIRECTIONS: Questions 15 through 17 are to be answered SOLELY on the basis of the following passage.

Some early psychologists believed that the basic characteristic of the criminal type was inferiority of intelligence, if not outright feeblemindedness. They were misled by the fact that they had measurements for all kinds of criminals, but, until World War I gave them a draft army sample, they had no information on a comparable group of non-criminal adults. As soon as acceptable measurements could be taken of criminals and a comparable group of non-criminals, concern with feeblemindedness or with low intelligence as a type took on less and less significance in research in criminology.

15. According to the above passage, some early psychologists were in error because they didn't 15.____
    A. distinguish among the various types of criminals
    B. devise a suitable method of measuring intelligence
    C. measure the intelligence of non-criminals as a basis for comparison

D. distinguish between feeblemindedness and inferiority of intelligence
E. clearly define the term *intelligence*

16. The above passage implies that studies of the intelligence of criminals and non-criminals
    A. are useless because it is impossible to obtain comparable groups
    B. are not meaningful because only the less intelligent criminals are detected
    C. indicate that criminals are more intelligent than non-criminals
    D. indicate that criminals are less intelligent than non-criminals
    E. do not indicate that there are any differences between the two groups

16.____

17. According to the above passage, studies of the World War I draft gave psychologists vital information concerning
    A. adaptability to army life of criminals and non-criminals
    B. criminal tendencies among draftees
    C. the intelligence scores of large numbers of men
    D. differences between intelligence scores of draftees and volunteers
    E. the behavior of men under abnormal conditions

17.____

Questions 18-20.

DIRECTIONS: Questions 18 through 20 are to be answered SOLELY on the basis of the following passage.

The use of a roadblock is simply an adaptation to police practices of the military concept of encirclement. Successful operation of a roadblock plan depends almost entirely on the amount of advance study and planning given to such operations. A thorough and detailed examination of the roads and terrain under the jurisdiction of a given policy agency should be made with the locations of the roadblocks pinpointed in advance. The first principle to be borne in mind in the location of each roadblock is the time element. Its location must be at a point beyond which the fugitive could not have possibly traveled in the time elapsed from the commission of the crime to the arrival of the officers at the roadblock.

18. According to the above passage,
    A. military operations have made extensive use of roadblocks
    B. the military concept of encirclement is an adaptation of police use of roadblocks
    C. the technique of encirclement has been widely used by military forces
    D. a roadblock is generally more effective than encirclement
    E. police use of roadblocks is based on the idea of military encirclement

18.____

19. According to the above passage,
    A. the factor of time is the sole consideration in the location of a roadblock
    B. the maximum speed possible in the method of escape is of major importance in roadblock location
    C. the time of arrival of officers at the site of a proposed roadblock is of little importance

19.____

D. if the method of escape is not known, it should be assumed that the escape is by automobile
E. a roadblock should be sited as close to the scene of the crime as the terrain will permit

20. According to the above passage, 20._____
    A. advance study and planning are of minor importance in the success of roadblock operations
    B. a thorough and detailed examination of all roads within a radius of fifty miles should precede the determination of a roadblock location
    C. consideration of terrain features are important in planning the location of roadblocks
    D. the pinpointing of roadblocks should be performed before any advance study is made
    E. a roadblock operation can seldom be successfully undertaken by a single police agency

KEY (CORRECT ANSWERS)

1.	B	11.	C
2.	D	12.	C
3.	A	13.	D
4.	C	14.	B
5.	B	15.	C
6.	A	16.	E
7.	A	17.	C
8.	E	18.	E
9.	B	19.	B
10.	D	20.	C

TEST 2

DIRECTIONS: Each question or incomplete statement is followed by several suggested answers or completions. Select the one that BEST answers the question or completes the statement. *PRINT THE LETTER OF THE CORRECT ANSWER IN THE SPACE AT THE RIGHT.*

Questions 1-3.

DIRECTIONS: Questions 1 through 3 are to be answered SOLELY on the basis of the following passage.

    Modern police science may be said to have three phases. The first phase embraces the identification of living and dead persons. The second embraces the field work carried out by specially trained detectives at the scene of the crime. The third embraces methods used in the police laboratory to examine and analyze clues and traces discovered in the course of the investigation. While modern police science has had a striking influence on detective work and will surely further enhance its effectiveness, the time-honored methods and practical detective work will always be important. The time-honored methods, that is knowledge of methods used by criminals, patience, tact, industry, thoroughness, and imagination, will always be requisites for successful detective work.

1. According to the above passage, we may expect modern police science to   1.____
   - A. help detective work more and more
   - B. become more and more scientific
   - C. depend less and less on the time-honored methods
   - D. bring together the many different approaches to detective work
   - E. play a less important role in detective work

2. According to the above passage, a knowledge of the procedures used by criminals is   2.____
   - A. solely an element of the modern police science approach to detective work
   - B. related to the identification of persons
   - C. not related to detective field work
   - D. related to methods used in the police laboratory
   - E. an element of the traditional approach to detective work

3. Modern police science and practical detective work, according to the above passage,   3.____
   - A. when used together can only lead to confusion
   - B. are based distinctly different theories of detective work
   - C. have had strikingly different influence on detective work
   - D. should both be used for successful detective work
   - E. lead usually to similar results

Questions 4-7.

DIRECTIONS: Questions 4 through 7 are to be answered SOLELY on the basis of the following passage.

A member of the force shall render reasonable aid to a sick or injured person. He shall summon an ambulance, if necessary, by telephoning the communications bureau of the borough, who shall notify the precinct concerned. If possible, he shall wait in full view of the arriving ambulance and take necessary action to direct the responding doctor or attendant to the patient, without delay. If the ambulance does not arrive in twenty minutes, he shall send in a second call. However, if the sick person is in his or her own home, a member of the force, before summoning an ambulance, will ascertain whether such person is willing to be taken to a hospital for treatment.

4. According to the above passage, if a patrolman wants to get an ambulance for a sick person, he should telephone
    A. the precinct concerned
    B. only if the sick person is in his home
    C. the nearest hospital
    D. only if the sick person is not in his home
    E. the borough communications bureau

5. According to the above passage, if a patrolman telephones for an ambulance and none arrives within twenty minutes, he should
    A. ask the injured person if he is willing to be taken to a hospital
    B. call the borough communications bureau
    C. call the precinct concerned
    D. attempt to give the injured person such assistance as he may need
    E. call the nearest hospital

6. A patrolman is called to help a woman who has fallen in her own home and has apparently broken her leg.
   According to the above passage, he should
    A. ask her if she wants to go to a hospital
    B. try to set her leg if it is necessary
    C. call for an ambulance at once
    D. attempt to get a doctor as quickly as possible
    E. not attempt to help the woman in any way before competent medical aid arrives

7. A man falls from a window into the backyard of an apartment house. Assume that you are a patrolman and that you are called to assist this man.
   According to the above passage, after you have called for an ambulance and comforted the injured man as much as you can, you should
    A. wait in front of the house for the ambulance
    B. ask the injured man if he wishes to go to the hospital for treatment
    C. remain with the injured man until the ambulance arrives
    D. send a bystander to direct the nearest doctor to the patient
    E. not ask the man to explain how the accident happened

Questions 8-10.

DIRECTIONS: Questions 8 through 10 are to be answered SOLELY on the basis of the following passage.

What is required is a program that will protect our citizens and their property from criminal and antisocial acts, will effectively restrain and reform juvenile delinquents, and will prevent the further development of antisocial behavior. Discipline and punishment of offenders must necessarily play an important part in any such program. Serious offenders cannot be mollycoddled merely because they are under twenty-one. Restraint and punishment necessarily follow serious antisocial acts. But punishment, if it is to be effective, must be a planned part of a more comprehensive program of treating delinquency.

8. The one of the following goals NOT included among those listed above is to
   A. stop young people from defacing public property
   B. keep homes from being broken into
   C. develop an intra-city boys' baseball league
   D. change juvenile delinquents into useful citizens
   E. prevent young people from developing antisocial behavior patterns

8.____

9. According to the above passage, punishment is
   A. not satisfactory in any program dealing with juvenile delinquents
   B. the most effective means by which young vandals and hooligans can be reformed
   C. not used sufficiently when dealing with serious offenders who are under twenty-one
   D. of value in reducing juvenile delinquency only if it is part of a complete program
   E. most effective when it does not relate to specific antisocial acts

9.____

10. With respect to serious offenders who are under twenty-one, the above passage suggests that they
    A. be mollycoddled
    B. be dealt with as part of a comprehensive program to punish mature criminals
    C. should be punished
    D. be prevented, by brute force if necessary, from performing antisocial acts
    E. be treated as delinquent children who require more love than punishment

10.____

Questions 11-14.

DIRECTIONS: Questions 11 through 14 are to be answered SOLELY on the basis of the following passage.

In all cases of homicide, members of the Police Department who investigate will make every effort to obtain statements from dying persons. Such statements are of the greatest importance to the District Attorney. In many cases, there may be a failure to solve the crime if they are not taken. The principle element to be considered in taking the declaration of a dying person is his mental attitude. In order to be admissible in evidence, the person must have no hope of recovery. The patient will be fully interrogated on that point before a statement is taken.

11. In cases of homicide, according to the above passage, members of the police force will
    A. try to change the mental attitude of the dying person
    B. attempt to obtain a statement from the dying person
    C. not give the information they obtain directly to the District Attorney
    D. be careful not to injure the dying person unnecessarily
    E. prevent unauthorized persons from taking dying declarations

12. The mental attitude of the person making the dying statement is of great importance because it can determine, according to the above passage, whether the
    A. victim should be interrogated in the presence of witnesses
    B. victim will be willing to make a statement of any kind
    C. victim has been forced to make the statement
    D. statement will tell the District Attorney who committed the crime
    E. statement can be used as evidence

13. District Attorneys find that statements of a dying person are important, according to the above passage, because
    A. it may be that the victim will recover and refuse to testify
    B. they are important elements in determining the mental attitude of the victim
    C. they present a point of view
    D. it may be impossible to punish the criminal without such a statement
    E. dead men tell no tales

14. A well-known gangster is found dying from a bullet wound. The patrolman first on the scene, in the presence of witnesses, tells the man that he is going to die and asks, *Who shot you?* The gangster says, *Jones shot me, but he hasn't killed me. I'll live to get him.* He then falls back dead.
    According to the above passage, this statement is
    A. *admissible* in evidence; the man was obviously speaking the truth
    B. *not admissible* in evidence; the man obviously did not believe that he was dying
    C. *admissible* in evidence; there were witnesses to the statement
    D. *not admissible* in evidence; the victim did not sign any statement and the evidence is merely hearsay
    E. *admissible* in evidence; there was no time to interrogate the victim

Questions 15-17.

DIRECTIONS: Questions 15 through 17 are to be answered SOLELY on the basis of the following passage.

The factors contributing to crime and delinquency are varied and complex. The home and its immediate environment have been found to be crucial in determining the behavior patterns of the individual, and criminality can frequently be traced to faulty family relationships and a bad neighborhood. But in the search for a clearer understanding of the underlying causes of delinquent and criminal behavior, the total environment must be taken into consideration.

15. According to the above passage, family relationships   15.____
    A. tend to become faulty in bad neighborhoods
    B. are important in determining the actions of honest people as well as criminals
    C. are the only important element in the understanding of causes of delinquency
    D. are determined by the total environment
    E. of criminals are understandable only in terms of the behavior patterns of the individuals concerned

16. According to the above passage, the causes of crime and delinquency are   16.____
    A. not simple   B. not meaningless
    C. meaningless   D. simple
    E. always understandable

17. According to the above passage, faulty family relationships frequently are   17.____
    A. responsible for varied and complex results
    B. caused by differences
    C. caused when one or both parents have a criminal behavior pattern
    D. independent of the total environment
    E. the cause of criminal acts

Questions 18-20.

DIRECTIONS: Questions 18 through 20 are to be answered SOLELY on the basis of the following passage.

A change in the specific problems which confront the police and in the methods for dealing with them has taken place in the last few decades. The automobile is a two-way symbol of this change in policing. It menaces every city with a complicated traffic problem and has speeded up the process of committing a crime and making a getaway, but at the same time has increased the effectiveness of police operations. However, the major concern of police departments continues to be the antisocial or criminal actions and behavior of human beings.

18. On the basis of the above passage, it can be stated that for the most part in   18.____
    the past few decades, the specific problems of a police force
    A. have changed but the general problems have not
    B. as well as the general problems have changed
    C. have remained the same but the general problems have changed
    D. as well as the general problems have remained the same
    E. have caused changes in the general problems

19. According to the above passage, advances in science and industry have, in general, made the police
    A. operations less effective from the overall point of view
    B. operations more effective from the overall point of view
    C. abandon older methods of solving police problems
    D. concern themselves more with the antisocial acts of human beings
    E. concern themselves less with the antisocial acts of human beings

20. The automobile is a *two-way symbol*, according to the above passage, because its use
    A. has speeded up getting to, and away from, the scene of a crime
    B. both helps and hurts police operations
    C. introduces a new antisocial act—traffic violation—and does away with criminals like horse thieves
    D. both increases and decreases speed by introducing traffic problems
    E. helps people get to the city but prevents them from moving once they are there

KEY (CORRECT ANSWERS)

1.	A	11.	B
2.	E	12.	E
3.	D	13.	D
4.	E	14.	B
5.	B	15.	B
6.	A	16.	A
7.	A	17.	E
8.	C	18.	A
9.	D	19.	B
10.	C	20.	B

PREPARING WRITTEN MATERIALS
EXAMINATION SECTION
TEST 1

DIRECTIONS: Each question consists of a sentence which may be classified appropriately under one of the following four categories:
- A. Incorrect because of faulty grammar or sentence structure.
- B. Incorrect because of faulty punctuation.
- C. Incorrect because of faulty spelling or capitalization.
- D. Correct

Examine each sentence carefully. Then, in the space at the right, print the capital letter preceding the option which is the BEST of the four suggested above. All incorrect sentences contain only one type of error. Consider a sentence correct if it contains none of the types of errors mentioned, although there may be other correct ways of expressing the same thought.

1. The fire apparently started in the storeroom, which is usually locked. 1._____
2. On approaching the victim two bruises were noticed by this officer. 2._____
3. The officer, who was there examined the report with great care. 3._____
4. Each employee in the office had a separate desk. 4._____
5. The suggested procedure is similar to the one now in use. 5._____
6. No one was more pleased with the new procedure than the chauffeur. 6._____
7. He tried to pursuade her to change the procedure. 7._____
8. The total of the expenses charged to petty cash were high. 8._____
9. An understanding between him and I was finally reached. 9._____
10. It was at the supervisor's request that the clerk agreed to postpone his vacation. 10._____
11. We do not believe that it is necessary for both he and the clerk to attend the conference. 11._____
12. All employees, who display perseverance, will be given adequate recognition. 12._____
13. He regrets that some of us employees are dissatisfied with our new assignments. 13._____

14. "Do you think that the raise was merited," asked the supervisor? 14._____

15. The new manual of procedure is a valuable supplament to our rules and regulation. 15._____

16. The typist admitted that she had attempted to pursuade the other employees to assist her in her work. 16._____

17. The supervisor asked that all amendments to the regulations be handled by you and I. 17._____

18. They told both he and I that the prisoner had escaped. 18._____

19. Any superior officer, who, disregards the just complaints of his subordinates, is remiss in the performance of his duty. 19._____

20. Only those members of the national organization who resided in the Middle west attended the conference in Chicago. 20._____

21. We told him to give the investigation assignment to whoever was available. 21._____

22. Please do not disappoint and embarass us by not appearing in court. 22._____

23. Despite the efforts of the Supervising mechanic, the elevator could not be started. 23._____

24. The U.S. Weather Bureau, weather record for the accident date was checked. 24._____

KEY (CORRECT ANSWERS)

1.	D	11.	A
2.	A	12.	B
3.	B	13.	D
4.	D	14.	B
5.	D	15.	C
6.	D	16.	C
7.	C	17.	A
8.	A	18.	A
9.	A	19.	B
10.	D	20.	C

21. D
22. C
23. C
24. B

TEST 2

DIRECTIONS: Each question consists of a sentence. Some of the sentences contain errors in English grammar or usage, punctuation, spelling, or capitalization. A sentence does not contain an error simply because it could be written in a different manner. Choose answer:
   A. If the sentence contains an error in English grammar or usage.
   B. if the sentence contains an error in punctuation.
   C. If the sentence contains an error in spelling or capitalization
   D. If the sentence does not contain any errors.

1. The severity of the sentence prescribed by contemporary statutes—including both the former and the revised New York Penal Laws—do not depend on what crime was intended by the offender.   1._____

2. It is generally recognized that two defects in the early law of attempt played a part in the birth of burglary: (1) immunity from prosecution for conduct short of the last act before completion of the crime, and (2) the relatively minor penalty imposed for an attempt (it being a common law misdemeanor) vis-à-vis the completed offense.   2._____

3. The first sentence of the statute is applicable to employees who enter their place of employment, invited guests, and all other persons who have an express or implied license or privilege to enter the premises.   3._____

4. Contemporary criminal codes in the United States generally divide burglary into various degrees, differentiating the categories according to place, time and other attendent circumstances.   4._____

5. The assignment was completed in record time but the payroll for it has not yet been prepaid.   5._____

6. The operator, on the other hand, is willing to learn me how to use the mimeograph.   6._____

7. She is the prettiest of the three sisters.   7._____

8. She doesn't know; if the mail has arrived.   8._____

9. The doorknob of the office door is broke.   9._____

10. Although the department's supply of scratch pads and stationery have diminished considerably, the allotment for our division has not been reduced.   10._____

11. You have not told us whom you wish to designate as your secretary.   11._____

12. Upon reading the minutes of the last meeting, the new proposal was taken up for consideration.   12._____

2 (#2)

13. Before beginning the discussion, we locked the door as a precautionery measure. 13._____

14. The supervisor remarked, "Only those clerks, who perform routine work, are permitted to take a rest period." 14._____

15. Not only will this duplicating machine make accurate copies, but it will also produce a quantity of work equal to fifteen transcribing typists. 15._____

16. "Mr. Jones," said the supervisor, "we regret our inability to grant you an extention of your leave of absence." 16._____

17. Although the employees find the work monotonous and fatigueing, they rarely complain. 17._____

18. We completed the tabulation of the receipts on time despite the fact that Miss Smith our fastest operator was absent for over a week. 18._____

19. The reaction of the employees who attended the meeting, as well as the reaction of those who did not attend, indicates clearly that the schedule is satisfactory to everyone concerned. 19._____

20. Of the two employees, the one in our office is the most efficient. 20._____

21. No one can apply or even understand, the new rules and regulations. 21._____

22. A large amount of supplies were stored in the empty office. 22._____

23. If an employee is occassionally asked to work overtime, he should do so willingly. 23._____

24. It is true that the new procedures are difficult to use but, we are certain that you will learn them quickly. 24._____

25. The office manager said that he did not know who would be given a large allotment under the new plan. 25._____

KEY (CORRECT ANSWERS)

1. A
2. D
3. D
4. C
5. C

6. A
7. D
8. B
9. A
10. A

11. D
12. A
13. C
14. B
15. A

16. C
17. C
18. B
19. D
20. A

21. B
22. A
23. C
24. B
25. D

TEST 3

DIRECTIONS: Each of the following sentences may be classified MOST appropriately under one of the following categories:
  A. Faulty because of incorrect grammar
  B. Faulty because of incorrect punctuation
  C. Faulty because of incorrect capitalization
  D. Correct

Examine each sentence carefully. Then, in the space at the right, print the capital letter preceding the option which is the BEST of the four suggested above. All incorrect sentence contain but one type of error. Consider a sentence correct if it contains none of the types of errors mentioned, even though there may be other correct ways of expressing the same thought.

1. The desk, as well as the chairs, were moved out of the office. 1.____

2. The clerk whose production was greatest for the month won a day's vacation as first prize. 2.____

3. Upon entering the room, the employees were found hard at work at their desks. 3.____

4. John Smith our new employee always arrives at work on time. 4.____

5. Punish whoever is guilty of stealing the money. 5.____

6. Intelligent and persistent effort lead to success no matter what the job may be. 6.____

7. The secretary asked, "can you call again at three o'clock?" 7.____

8. He told us, that if the report was not accepted at the next meeting, it would have to be rewritten. 8.____

9. He would not have sent the letter if he had known that it would cause so much excitement. 9.____

10. We all looked forward to him coming to visit us. 10.____

11. If you find that you are unable to complete the assignment please notify me as soon as possible. 11.____

12. Every girl in the office went home on time but me; there was still some work for me to finish. 12.____

13. He wanted to know who the letter was addressed to, Mr. Brown or Mr. Smith. 13.____

14. "Mr. Jones, he said, please answer this letter as soon as possible." 14.____

15. The new clerk had an unusual accent inasmuch as he was born and   15._____
    educated in the south.

16. Although he is younger than her, he earns a higher salary.   16._____

17. Neither of the two administrators are going to attend the conference being 17._____
    held in Washington, D.C.

18. Since Miss Smith and Miss Jones have more experience than us, they have 18._____
    been given more responsible duties.

19. Mr. Shaw the supervisor of the stock room maintains an inventory of stationery 19._____
    and office supplies.

20. Inasmuch as this matter affects both you and I, we should take joint action. 20._____

21. Who do you think will be able to perform this highly technical work? 21._____

22. Of the two employees, John is considered the most competent.   22._____

23. He is not coming home on tuesday; we expect him next week.   23._____

24. Stenographers, as well as typists must be able to type rapidly and accurately. 24._____

25. Having been placed in the safe we were sure that the money would not be 25._____
    stolen.

KEY (CORRECT ANSWERS)

1.	A	11.	B
2.	D	12.	D
3.	A	13.	A
4.	B	14.	B
5.	D	15.	C
6.	A	16.	A
7.	C	17.	A
8.	B	18.	A
9.	D	19.	B
10.	A	20.	A

21.	D
22.	A
23.	C
24.	B
25.	A

TEST 4

DIRECTIONS: Each of the following sentences consist of four sentences lettered A, B, C, and D. One of the sentences in each group contains an error in grammar or punctuation. Indicate the INCORRECT sentence in each group. *PRINT THE LETTER OF THE CORRECT ANSWER IN THE SPACE AT THE RIGHT.*

1. A. Give the message to whoever is on duty.
   B. The teacher who's pupil won first prize presented the award.
   C. Between you and me, I don't expect the program to succeed.
   D. His running to catch the bus caused the accident.

   1.____

2. A. The process, which was patented only last year is already obsolete.
   B. His interest in science (which continues to the present) led him to convert his basement into a laboratory.
   C. He described the book as "verbose, repetitious, and bombastic".
   D. Our new director will need to possess three qualities: vision, patience, and fortitude.

   2.____

3. A. The length of ladder trucks varies considerably.
   B. The probationary fireman reported to the officer to who he was assigned.
   C. The lecturer emphasized the need for we firemen to be punctual.
   D. Neither the officers nor the members of the company knew about the new procedure.

   3.____

4. A. Ham and eggs is the specialty of the house.
   B. He is one of the students who are on probation.
   C. Do you think that either one of us have a chance to be nominated for president of the class?
   D. I assume that either he was to be in charge or you were.

   4.____

5. A. Its a long road that has no turn.
   B. To run is more tiring than to walk.
   C. We have been assigned three new reports: namely, the statistical summary, the narrative summary, and the budgetary summary.
   D. Had the first payment been made in January, the second would be due in April.

   5.____

6. A. Each employer has his own responsibilities.
   B. If a person speaks correctly, they make a good impression.
   C. Every one of the operators has had her vacation.
   D. Has anybody filed his report?

   6.____

7. A. The manager, with all his salesmen, was obliged to go.
   B. Who besides them is to sign the agreement?
   C. One report without the others is incomplete.
   D. Several clerks, as well as the proprietor, was injured.

   7.____

8. A. A suspension of these activities is expected.
    B. The machine is economical because first cost and upkeep are low.
    C. A knowledge of stenography and filing are required for this position.
    D. The condition in which the goods were received shows that the packing was not done properly.

9. A. There seems to be a great many reasons for disagreement.
    B. It does not seem possible that they could have failed.
    C. Have there always been too few applicants for these positions?
    D. There is no excuse for these errors.

10. A. We shall be pleased to answer your question.
    B. Shall we plan the meeting for Saturday?
    C. I will call you promptly at seven.
    D. Can I borrow your book after you have read it?

11. A. You are as capable as I.
    B. Everyone is willing to sign but him and me.
    C. As for he and his assistant, I cannot praise them too highly.
    D. Between you and me, I think he will be dismissed.

12. A. Our competitors bid above us last week.
    B. The survey which was began last year has not yet been completed.
    C. The operators had shown that they understood their instructions.
    D. We have never ridden over worse roads.

13. A. Who did they say was responsible?
    B. Whom did you suspect?
    C. Who do you suppose it was?
    D. Whom do you mean?

14. A. Of the two propositions, this is the worse.
    B. Which report do you consider the best   the one in January or the one in July?
    C. I believe this is the most practicable of the many plans submitted.
    D. He is the youngest employee in the organization.

15. A. The firm had but three orders last week.
    B. That doesn't really seem possible.
    C. After twenty years scarcely none of the old business remains.
    D. Has he done nothing about it?

KEY (CORRECT ANSWERS)

1.	B	6.	B	11.	C
2.	A	7.	D	12.	B
3.	C	8.	C	13.	A
4.	C	9.	A	14.	B
5.	A	10.	D	15.	C

REPORT WRITING
EXAMINATION SECTION
TEST 1

DIRECTIONS: Each question or incomplete statement is followed by several suggested answers or completions. Select the one that *BEST* answers the question or completes the statement. *PRINT THE LETTER OF THE CORRECT ANSWER IN THE SPACE AT THE RIGHT.*
Answer all questions *SOLELY* on the basis of the information contained in the report.

Questions 1-3.

DIRECTIONS: Questions 1 through 3 are based on the following report on a personnel matter concerning a member of the force. The report consists of thirty-eight numbered sentences and tabulated entries, some of which may not be correct or consistent with the principles of good police report writing.

1 Police Officer Morton, #3999, was appointed to this Department on 5/11/00. *2* A review of the officer's attendance record, since his appointment, reveals the following:

	Year	Number of Sick Calls	Total Tours Lost
3			
4	2000	2	3
5	2001	8	14
6	2002	9	13
7	2003	0	0
8	2004	6	9
9	2005	0	0
10	2006	20	63
11	2007 (to date)	12	26

12 The officer, since his appointment date, has been the subject of disciplinary action on eleven separate occasions. *13* The attendance record indicates that Police Officer Morton has reported late for duty a total of four times since being assigned to this patrol division. *14* Listed below is a summary of Police Officer Morton's disciplinary history with the Department:

	Date	Charge	Finding	Local Trial Penalty
15				
16	5/4/01	Off post	Guilty	Reprimand
17	6/6/02	Out of uniform	Guilty	1 day annual leave
18	9/4/02	Improper patrol	Guilty	5 days annual leave
19	8/20/04	Improper time sheet	Guilty	Reprimand
20	10/13/04	Lost shield	Guilty	2 days suspension
21	11/3/04	Not home on sick report	Guilty	1 day's pay
22	5/26/05	Improper blotter entries	Guilty	$25 fine
23	6/2/05	Off post	Not Guilty	----
24	4/10/06	Lost revolver	Guilty	5 days suspension
25	2/3/07	Not home on sick report	Guilty	5 days suspension
26	6/1/07	Unfit for duty	Pending	----

107

27 Police Officer Morton's personnel folder indicates that he has been counseled on various occasions by superior officers of the Department. *28* It would appear that said counseling has been to no avail, other than the officer's interview in December 2004 by Sergeant Green of the Deputy Chief's office. *29* As a result of that interview, the officer's sick record improved considerably for the subsequent year. *30* Police Officer Morton has been the recipient of Departmental Recognition three times, and was awarded two Excellent Police Duties and one Authority Commendation. *31* His monthly activity record indicates that the officer performs an acceptable quantity of work when compared to his peer group. *32* The officer was interviewed by the undersigned this date. *33* His record was reviewed with him and inquiry was made by the undersigned as to the existence of personal problems or other factors which might be presented in mitigation of his poor record. *34* Police Officer Morton denied any personal problems and stated that "his record was not as bad as some other officers, he has been a frequent victim of circumstances, and by and large has been singled out for harassment by all superior officers of the Department." *35* It would appear to the undersigned that the officer has still not recognized or accepted his record as being poor, nor does he accept responsibility for it. *36* It would also appear to the undersigned that both individual counseling and numerous appearances before a local trial officer have not been effective in changing the officer's attitude. *37* Furthermore, the officer's job performance has never been more than satisfactory. *38* Based upon Police Officer Morton's overall record, it is the recommendation of the undersigned that this matter (Unfit for duty, 4/12/07, charges attached hereto) become the subject of a General Trial proceeding.

1. Which one of the following sentences or tabulated entries does *NOT* contain sufficient information?

   A. 3   B. 13   C. 28   D. 31

2. Which one of the following sentences or tabulated entries does *NOT* appear in its proper sequence in the report?

   A. 2   B. 12   C. 22   D. 35

3. Which one of the following sentences or tabulated entries contains material which is *contradicted* by other information given in the report?

   A. 6   B. 21   C. 36   D. 37

KEY (CORRECT ANSWERS)

1. B
2. B
3. D

TEST 2

Questions 1-5.

DIRECTIONS: Questions 1 through 5 are based on the following report of a Firearm Discharge by a member of the force. The report consists of 28 numbered sentences, some of which may not be correct or consistent with the principles of good police report writing.

1 Investigation reveals that Police Officer K fired 4 shots from his service revolver, S&W, .38 cal., serial #C574737. *2* Responded to place of occurrence, 420 E. 105 Street, Apartment 6F, East River Houses, N.Y., N.Y., arriving at 2240 hours. *3* Also present were Captain A, Commanding Officer, 23rd Precinct; Police Officer J; and Detectives Y & Z, N.Y.C. Police Department. *4* At 2200 hours this date received notification from Headquarters Desk Supervisor, Lieutenant L, that Police Officer K, #345, assigned to and performing duty at East River Houses, had discharged his firearm. *5* Upon arrival, conferred with Lieutenant X, Commanding Officer Sub-Division C, and Sergeant N, Patrol Bureau Relief, who were already on the scene. *6* Police Officer K, when interviewed, provided the following information:

7 While performing uniformed patrol duty at East River Houses on the third platoon, he responded to 402 E. 105th Street, apartment 6F, at 2140 hours this date. *8* Response was as a result of a radio message received from Central at 2130 hours this date of an anonymous complaint of a dispute at the location. *9* The officer was performing the second tour in a set of four tours of duty on the third platoon. *10* He responded alone because Police Officer F, #291, also scheduled for duty on the third platoon at East River Houses, had called on sick report. *11* As he entered the apartment he observed Mrs. Theresa Miller, F/W/26, resident of apartment 6F, 420 E. 105 Street, (T) East River Houses, engaged in a physical struggle with one Harold Wilson (NT) M/W/22, of 658 New Jersey Avenue, Brooklyn, N.Y., and his wife, Harriet Wilson, F/W/21, same address. *12* The officer separated the combatants and restored order. *13* The female advised Police Officer K that the basis for the dispute was a failure to pay a debt owed. *14* All parties agreed not to file criminal complaints and Mr. and Mrs. Wilson started to leave the apartment. *15* At this point, Mrs. Miller withdrew a .22 calibre Rohm revolver, serial #3015, from her apron pocket and pointed it at the departing officer and the Wilsons. *16* Police Officer K, in the foyer of the apartment, turned and cautioned Mrs. Miller to drop the gun.

17 The Wilsons, observing Mrs. Miller's actions, fled the apartment. *18* Police Officer K again asked Mrs. Miller to drop the gun, whereupon she fired three shots at the officer. *19* All three shots missed, two striking the apartment door behind the officer and one, the foyer wall. *20* Police Officer K returned the fire, discharging his revolver four times.

21 All four bullets struck Mrs. Miller, two in the right arm, one in the left arm, and one in the right ankle. *22* Mr. and Mrs. Wilson, when interviewed, corroborated the police officer's version of the incident up to the point of their departure from the apartment. *23* The Wilsons then heard numerous gun shots and ran for help. *24* Both agreed that the officer's actions were most appropriate, based upon their observations of the incident.

25 Mrs. Miller was removed to Metropolitan Hospital and she was confined there in a stable condition. *26* She will be charged with attempted murder and possession of a deadly weapon. *27* Police Officer K's revolver was checked by Sergeant N and found to contain two live and four spent rounds.

28 It is the opinion of the undersigned that Police Officer K fired his revolver in accordance with the applicable laws of the State of New York and in compliance with the rules and policies of this Department.

1. Of the following, which would be the MOST logical sequence for the first five sentences of the report?

    A. 2,5,1,3,4
    B. 2, 4,1,5, 3
    C. 4,2,5,3,1
    D. 4, 2,1,3, 5

2. Which one of the following sentences contains a conclusion rather than a statement of fact?

    A. 16
    B. 19
    C. 22
    D. 24

3. Which one of the following sentences from the report is written in such a manner as to be *ambiguous*?

    A. 8
    B. 10
    C. 13
    D. 26

4. Which one of the following sentences from the report contains material which is CONTRADICTED by other information given in the report?

    A. 7
    B. 15
    C. 21
    D. 28

5. Which one of the following sentences from the report contains material which is LEAST relevant to this report?

    A. 9
    B. 10
    C. 18
    D. 25

KEY (CORRECT ANSWERS)

1. C
2. D
3. C
4. A
5. A

TEST 3

DIRECTIONS: Each question or incomplete statement is followed by several suggested answers or completions. Select the one that BEST answers the question or completes the statement. PRINT THE LETTER OF THE CORRECT ANSWER IN THE SPACE AT THE RIGHT.

1 Lieutenant John Carlson, Commanding Officer of Sub-Division Z, arrived at 300 Adam St., apt. 14 B in Charles Houses, at 1645 hours, on 12/6/ . *2* Present at that time were Mary Brown, F/B/14, who had apparently suffered lacerations of the head, Mrs. Elizabeth Brown, F/B/40, mother of Mary, and P.O. James Deere #4012 assigned to Charles Houses. *3* Mrs. Brown resides in the building, 300 Adam St., apt. 14B, with her daughter and husband, Joseph Brown, who was not present at the scene. *4* Mr. Brown was at work at the Squire Bottling Plant where he is employed as a plant shift supervisor. *5* While awaiting the arrival of the ambulance, P.O. Deere interviewed Mrs. Brown, who was obviously distraught, though uninjured. *6* Mrs. Brown stated that, at approximately 1635 hours, just after the bottle struck her daughter, she looked up and saw two male youths, who had obviously thrown the bottle, duck back from a stairhall window. *7* She further stated that she had no idea who the boys were, although she had seen them before. *8* The ambulance arrived and removed Miss Brown, accompanied by her mother, to Metropolitan Hospital. *9* Attendant George Fuentes stated that Elizabeth Brown had sustained extensive scalp lacerations, but that no other serious symptoms were manifest. *10* A complete diagnosis will be obtained from the attending physician at Morrisania Hospital. *11* A subsequent interview of Stanley Wilson, H.A. caretaker employed at Charles Houses, was conducted in the Maintenance Office at 1725 hours. *12* Mr. Wilson stated that he saw two young males run from the rear exit at 300 Adam St. just after he had heard the crash of breaking glass and the shouts from the front of the building. *13* P.O. Deere asked Mr. Wilson if he had observed anyone who might have been involved in the bottle-throwing incident.
14 Mr. Wilson furnished a description of the two possible witnesses or participants. *15* No other persons interviewed observed youths fleeing from the building.

1. Which one of the following sentences is NOT relevant to the investigation? 1.____
   A. 4   B. 5   C. 7   D. 10

2. Which one of the following sentences contains information which is contradicted by other information given in the report? 2.____
   A. 9   B. 11   C. 14   D. 15

3. Which one of the following sentences is NOT in proper sequence? 3.____
   A. 5   B. 6   C. 10   D. 13

4. Which one of the following sentences contains information which is inconsistent with other information given in the report? 4.____
   A. A. 3   B. 6   C. 7   D. 8

KEY (CORRECT ANSWERS)

1. A
2. A
3. D
4. D

CAMPUS SECURITY

COMMENTARY

This section describes the structure of the campus security office and appraises its function through an examination of its legal apparatus and by the relationships it has maintained with other components of institutional life.

The findings are based upon research in the legal status of the security office and the authority of the security officer; questions as to the structure, the functioning, and the relationships of the security office; and the assessment of the campus security function and its ability to be supportive to students.

In particular, this summary takes cognizance of the inconsequential role heretofore delegated to the security officer and the significant part he may yet play as the threat to the security of the campus accelerates.

1. The history of the campus security office reflects a variety of service tasks distributed among several functionaries which ultimately came to be housed together. From the early fire-watching days to traffic control and student disorder, it has been a body generally utilized "for" but rarely considered "of" the university. Campus security officers and their predecessors have been long cast in roles of menial activities with minimal responsibilities. Never having attained recognition and legitimacy as a part of the total university community, they continue to exercise an uncertain authority amidst a questioning constituency.
2. The uncertainty that has always surrounded the role of the campus security officer is best evidenced in the limitations placed upon his authority. Until recent years few of the state legislatures bestowed direct arrest authority upon a campus security officer. The authority was obtained derivatively as a result of deputization by the local municipal police department or by the sheriff. Although many state legislatures now permit the governing bodies of higher education, such as the boards of regents, to designate campus security officers with peace officers' authority, deputization continues.
3. This situation exists inasmuch as the authority obtained through the governing bodies is usually of a narrow range and it has not yet had the benefit of adequate court testing and judicial approval. Some few states permit private colleges to obtain similar appointments, generally through application to the governor, but the rule among private colleges has been to rely on deputization for their campus security authority.
4. Among the states requiring mandatory training for entering police officers, several do not yet consider a campus security officer subject to the standards imposed upon peace officers. Moreover, the federal government specifically excludes many campus security officers from the benefits of available training scholarships. Virtually no organized, state-wide specialized training programs for campus security officers are either required under the law or are afforded under state auspices.
5. The law is well established in regard the right of institutions of higher educations to control traffic and parking within their own disciplinary machinery. The courts have upheld the colleges' imposition of reasonable penalties for such violations and have provided the civil court system as an appeal tribunal.
6. Adequate legal precedent exists upon which a campus security officer may enter a residence hall in search of contraband without benefit of a search warrant. The

case law condoning such entry is predicated upon several theories. The major legal premise is that the institution must be afforded the flexibility of access to all buildings in order to properly govern itself. The student is also considered only a temporary occupant of the premises and by his enrollment "waives" certain rights. The privilege of entry is available to administrators and may be delegated to law enforcement officers in the pursuit of a reasonable investigation. The erosion of the "in loco parentis" doctrine and recent judicial pronouncements suggest that the privilege of entry without a warrant may not be arbitrarily invoked.

7. The formalized role of the campus security office in major stress situations such as organized or spontaneous campus disorder is to provide intelligence upon which administrators may make decisions, to serve as liaison with outside police agencies, and to gather evidence for later use against students violating the law. Although the press of events may force campus security officers into confrontation situations, the plans for responding to campus disorders do not generally contemplate such a role. The campus security office's early involvement is aimed primarily at delay so that student personnel officers and the executive officer may have the opportunity to use whatever personal, persuasive influence they can marshal. In the event the institutional executive determines that outside force is necessary, the campus security serves as a communications liaison to interpret the tactical decisions demanded by the outside police agencies in terms of the goals aspired to by the executive.

8. While the complexities of a campus-wide disorder may impose limitations upon the involvement of the security officer, his ability to respond to the normal, foreseeable, routine, enforcement contingencies also remains open to question. The profile of the campus security function discloses many characteristics that suggest only a minimal ability to satisfy ordinary campus needs.

9. Particularly among small institutions and especially private colleges, the training is limited, the equipment is meager, and the advantages over the local police nonexistent. The security force generally lacks specialists within the department, has a minimum of sophisticated equipment, and what little intelligence is available is obtained from outside police sources. Students and female officers are scarcely used and only in short demand.

10. All components of the university recognize that the campus security force most effectively performs the tasks requiring the least specialty training. Building and ground patrol, parking, and traffic control are at the top rank, in that order, while the duties involving criminal investigation and student disorders are the areas least effectively performed.

11. It is apparent to security officers that the presence of larger student bodies, more vehicles on campus, more buildings to patrol, a rise in the individual crime rate, and the potential for disorder arising from student demonstrations call for an increased professional staff.

12. Administrative changes are sought by security officers with almost 60.0 percent favoring a centralized, state-wide coordinating body and almost 70.0 percent requesting a chain of command which would lead directly to the president. None of the other respondent groups (faculty, students, administrators) evinces strong support for these propositions.

13. There is no consensus among the campus groups as to the personnel changes which would most improve performance. The security officers and the administrators ranked salary increase as the top priority personnel change, whereas the students and the faculty selected specialized training in human behavior as their first

choice. Inasmuch as the campus security office services a select clientele in a unique setting, the projected changes need not be weighed against the prototype sought for the law enforcement officer employed to exercise order among the general population.

14. The campus security office has virtually no involvement in policy-making beyond traffic regulations and has little contact in a formal setting with students and faculty. A good working relationship seems to exist with the office of student affairs and other administrators as well as with the outside police agencies.

15. The strong support indicated by all four groups (campus security, faculty, students, and administrators) for the proposition that too few channels of communication exist between the campus security office and the students is evidenced by the lack of security officer participation in student educational programs, by the failure of the campus security office to meet regularly with student committees, and by the security office's absence in the process of establishing student codes of conduct and student discipline procedures. Students involved in off-campus arrests cannot look for security office assistance except to a small extent at schools in the under-10,000 population brackets.

16. Although administrative support for the campus security office as a policy-making body is absent, there is evidence showing regular committee meetings with the office of student affairs and other administration groups. A continuing exchange of information exists with the office of student affairs concerning problem students, and a concurring belief is held by all four groups that the administrators and the office of student affairs would support the action of the campus security office in a disorder situation.

17. The working relationship with administrators also extends to outside police agencies. The local police are available for many manpower and investigative services, and, in some instances, campus violations of the municipal and state law may be handled by security officers within the framework of the school's discipline structure rather than requiring students to face criminal prosecution. Despite the amicable ties between the campus security force and the local police, the security officer joined with the other three groups in unequivocally asserting that the over-reaction by outside police agencies was the occurrence most likely to change an orderly student demonstration into a campus disorder.

18. The aspirations of the campus security officer to contribute to the educational goals of the institution and to participate in its traditional customs finds little of a responsive chord among other components on campus. Although 40.0 percent of the security officers considered the aiding of students in the educational process as an appropriate goal, only 18.0 percent of the students and 6.0 percent of the faculty voiced agreement. The campus security officer viewed himself as the interpreter of the function of police agencies in our society, but the concept had only scattered support with the students and the faculty.

19. There was mixed sentiment toward the campus security officer's enforcement role. Some of the characteristics deemed the antithesis of higher education tradition were attributed to him. For instance, all of the groups identified him with an authoritarian enforcement approach. In addition, 50.0 percent of the student were critical of his use of informers and about 25.0 percent of all groups suggested that uniforms be replaced with civilian-like attire. Despite the 70.0 percent of the security officers seeking increased authority, there was a reluctance to increase campus security authority or to allow participation in student discipline policy-making. The suggestion that the campus security office is a policing agency and as such is

unacceptable to the academic community averaged but a 30.0 percent acceptance among all four groups. While the campus security office was not totally repudiated because of its law enforcement posture, nonetheless it has not been afforded peer status by the other components of the campus society.

20. The anticipation that a supportive relationship can be maintained with students while performing enforcement duties is an unfulfilled expectation. This was apparent to all four groups in their over-70.0 percent recognition that duties such as searching residence halls for contraband are inimical to maintaining a compatible association, and, as well, in their almost 50.0 percent recognition of the stress created in using necessary force against student disorders. Duties involving building and grounds patrol, traffic control, and criminal investigation are performed in less strained settings, permitting a more harmonious relationship.

21. The image of the campus security officer that is transmitted to the student represents order and authority. The uniform, the weapons, and the equipment are synonymous with discipline and control. From the student point of view, the product is not conducive to a mutuality of interest. The absence of joint educational programs and regularly scheduled committee meetings also negates the development of any meaningful interchange. The failure of campus security to offer assistance to students in need of aid as a result of an off-campus arrest may further estrange the two groups. The differential in educational background and age also widens the chasm.

22. Students do not go so far as to state that the campus security officer is too low in the status hierarchy to maintain their respect but they strongly favor supervisory controls such as student ombudsmen and a joint faculty-student committee to review the performance of the campus security officer.

23. The campus security officer as presently constituted is not trained to provide supportive services for students, is not given a status role by the administration which would engender a high regard, and does not participate in policy making or become involved in aspects of the educational process.

24. Little recognition is attainable to the security officer other than that arising from his enforcement activities. There are few if any common grounds existing between him and the student from which a symbiotic relationship may develop.

25. In some few critical areas, the results reflected similar percentage support among the four groups. However, the internal consistency check to determine agreement among the four groups within each institution showed that in only 2 of the 16 selected items were there affirmative responses suggesting consistent agreement within each of the schools. The item of greatest support had 82 of the 89 schools with all four groups agreeing to the truism that the campus security goal is to provide protection for property and person.

Fifty schools had all components in agreement that the overreaction by outside police agencies may change orderly demonstrations into a campus disorder. The other items showed considerably lower internal consistency scores. The diversity of attitude among the component groups that comprise the educational institutions of higher learning and the lack of unanimity within each institution suggest a searching reexamination of the campus security model.

BASIC FUNDAMENTALS OF INTERPERSONAL RELATIONSHIPS

TABLE OF CONTENTS

	Page
INSTRUCTIONAL OBJECTIVES	1
CONTENT	1
INTRODUCTION	1
1. Interpersonal Conduct and Behavior on the Job	1
Formal Organization of the Office	2
Office as a Setting for Formal and Informal Relations	2
Office Behavior	2
2. Interpersonal Communication – The Meaning	3
Importance of Face-to-Face Contacts	3
Listening Techniques	3
3. Factors in Interpersonal Communication	3
The Choice of Words of the Conversant	4
How Each Sees Each Other	4
The Right Time and Place	4
The Effect of Past Experience	4
The Effect of Personal Differences	5
4. Defense Mechanisms in Interpersonal Relations	5
Causes for Defense Mechanisms	5
Results of Use of Defense Mechanisms	5
5. Influences of Role Playing in Interpersonal Relations	6
Exploring Superior-Subordinate Relations	6
Interpersonal Relations Achieved Through Simulation	7
6. Measuring Interpersonal Relations	7
Survey of Interpersonal Values	7
Analysis of Interpersonal Behavior	8
STUDENT LEARNING ACTIVITIES	8
TEACHER MANAGEMENT ACTIVITIES	9
EVALUATION QUESTIONS	10

BASIC FUNDAMENTALS OF INTERPERSONAL RELATIONSHIPS

INSTRUCTIONAL OBJECTIVES

1. Ability to distinguish between formal and informal behavior.
2. Ability to identify the important factors in communicating with people.
3. Ability to understand how defense mechanisms affect communication with others.
4. Ability to identify the roles played in effective person-to-person communication.
5. Ability to acquire the human relations skills needed for getting along with others both on and off the job.
6. Ability to establish greater personal effectiveness with others so as to develop better cooperation and superior-subordinate relationships in public-service working situations.
7. Ability to recognize the mutual dependence of individuals on each other.
8. Ability to form positive attitudes toward the worth and dignity of every human being.
9. Ability to become aware of how feelings affect one's own behavior, as well as one's relationships with other people.
10. Ability to use an understanding of human relationships to effectively work with people.
11. Ability to improve communications with others by developing greater effectiveness in dealing with people in the world of public service.

CONTENT

INTRODUCTION

Perhaps the single most important skill that a public-service worker, or anyone for that matter, needs, is the ability to get along with other people. "Person-to-person" relationships are the building blocks of all social interactions between two-individuals. If there is one essential ingredient for success in life, both on and off the job, it is developing greater effectiveness in dealing with people.

The skill of the teacher is critical to the success of this unit. He should establish a permissive and non-threatening group climate in which free communication and behavior can take place. The importance of this unit cannot be over stated. The overall objective is to establish greater personal effectiveness with others and to develop better co-operative and superior-subordinate relationships in the public-service occupations. Obtaining greater "self-awareness" is a large part of this goal. Because interpersonal relations are affected by a variety of factors, some attention should be given initially to basic rules of conduct and behavior on the job.

1. INTERPERSONAL CONDUCT AND BEHAVIOR ON THE JOB

Most public-service agencies have clearly defined rules and regulations. The behavior of the public-service worker is often guided by the established procedures and directives of that individual agency. In many cases, even individual departments or units will have procedures manuals, which regulate conduct and office work.

Formal Organization of the Office

At one point or another, most public-service employees either work directly in an office, or come in frequent contact with other people working in an administrative or staff office. Students should become familiar with the organizational structure of the occupational groups in which they are planning on working. A park worker, for example, must know about the organization of the Parks Department—what kinds of staff or administrative services are provided, what about training, what are the safety rules, what goes into personnel records, etc. Preparing a flow chart of the relationships between different positions in a particular agency is one way of learning about the organization of that office or agency.

Office as a Setting for formal and Informal Relations

It is necessary to become aware of the different kinds of social relations shared with co-workers and the public. Some co-workers, for example, are seen only at work, and others are seen socially after work and/or on weekends. Factors that determine which co-workers become *personal* friends and which are just *work* friends should be considered and discussed.

On the other hand, a public-service worker usually has more formal relationships with the public with whom he comes into contact. Consider the relationships of the preschool teacher's aide and his students, the library helper and his library patrons, the police cadet and the general public, etc. In each of these cases, the public expects the public-service worker to help them with a particular service.

Although the distinction between formal and informal social relationships is not always clear, one should be sensitive to the fact that both kinds of relationships affect the behavior of the public and the public-service employee, Normally, the very organization of the public-service office helps to create a social climate for developing working relationships of a formal nature, and personal relationships with co-workers and the public which are of a more impersonal nature.

Office Behavior

Specific kinds of behavior relate to these formal and informal relationships with other people. Typically, the formal relationship is well prescribed and regulated by procedures or directives. The license interviewer, as an example, has specific questions to ask, and specific information to obtain from the applicant. Their relationship can be described as formal or prescribed by regulation. On the other hand, other office behavior can best be described as informal and non-prescribed (or *free*). Interpersonal relations in this case are often more personal and relaxed by their very nature.

2. INTERPERSONAL COMMUNICATION - THE MEANING

Interpersonal communication can be defined as a two-way flow of information from person-to-person. One cannot Study human relations without examining the constant relationships that man has with other people; the individual does not exist in a vacuum. Most of man's psychological and social needs are met through dealings with other people. In fact, one psychiatrist (Harry Stark Sullivan) has developed a theory of personality based upon interpersonal situations. This viewpoint, known as the *Interpersonal Theory of Psychiatry,* claims that personality is essentially the enduring pattern of continued interpersonal relationships between people. This interpersonal behavior is all that can be observed as personality.

Importance of Face-to-Face Contacts

The very phrase. *Public Service Occupations,* suggests frequent face-to-face contacts with not only the general public, but with co-workers as well. With possibly a few exceptions, practically every public-service employee encounters frequent person-to-person contacts both on and off the job. The ability to get along with people is a very important part of public-service work.

Listening Techniques

Effective listening is a critical part of interpersonal communications. Listening is an active process, requiring not only that one must *pay attention* to what is being said, but that one must also *listen* for the meaning of what is being said. Almost one-half of the total time spent communicating, (reading, writing, speaking, or listening) is spent in listening.

Even though people get considerable practice at listening, they don't do too well at it. Many studies have shown that, on the average, a person retains only about 25 percent of a given speech after only 10 minutes have elapsed. Most people forget three quarters of what they hear in a relatively short period of time. Clearly, people need to improve their listening skills if they are to become more effective in their relations with other people.

3. FACTORS IN INTERPERSONAL COMMUNICATION

There are a number of components that affect the person-to-person relationship. Some of the factors common to both the sender and the receiver in a person-to-person communication are:

The Attitudes and Emotions of the Individuals

For example - two people are shouting and screaming at each other - how effective is their interpersonal communication?

- *The Needs and Wants of the People Communicating*

Both the sender and receiver have unique desires, some open, and some hidden from the other person. These needs can and do strongly influence interpersonal relationships.

- *The Implied Demands of the Sender and Receiver*

  An important factor in interpersonal communications involves requests or demands. How are these demands handled? What are some typical responses to demands? These factors are common to both the sender and the receiver in interpersonal relations and affect the individual behavior of the people communicating.

The Choice of Words of the Conversant

One's choice of words can have a direct bearing on the interpersonal communication. The vocabulary one uses in interpersonal relationships should be appropriate for the occasion. For example, a preschool teacher's aide would not use the same vocabulary in talking to a three-year-old, as she would in talking to the preschool teacher.

How Each Sees the Other

The process of communicating from person-to-person is greatly influenced by the perception that the sender and receiver have of each other. The feelings that a person has toward the other person are reflected in his tone of voice, choice of words, and even in his *body language*. A reference book mentioned in the resource section of this unit, *How to Read a Person Like a Book,* deals with the importance of body language in person-to-person relationships.

The Right Time and Place

Another factor that may be important in interpersonal relationships is the timing of the communication. For example, one of the first things a supervisor should do if he wants to talk over a problem with his subordinate, is ask the question: "Is this the right time and place?" Problems should not generally be discussed in the middle of an office, where other employees, or the public, can hear the discussion. Personal problems should be discussed only in private.

The Effect of Past Experience

In general, the quality of the person-to-person transaction will depend upon the past experience of the individuals. Human beings have acquired most of their opinions, assumptions, and value judgments through their relationships with other people. Past experience not only helps to teach people about effective interpersonal relationships, it is also often responsible for the irrational prejudices that a person displays. A strong bias usually blocks the interpersonal relationship if the subject of the communication concerns that particular bias.

The Effect of Personal Differences

An additional factor in interpersonal communications involves the intelligence and other personal differences of the people communicating. An example of such a personal difference is the *objectivity* of the people involved, as compared with their *subjectivity*. One person may try to be very fair and objective in discussing a point with another person, yet this other person is, at the same time, taking everything personally and being very subjective in his viewpoint. It is almost as if an adult was talking to an angry child.

Such differences can impede the communications flow between two people. In fact, all the factors mentioned in communications should be examined as to whether they block or facilitate interpersonal relationships. *The most effective interpersonal relationships are those that are adult-like in their character.*

4. DEFENSE MECHANISMS IN INTERPERSONAL RELATIONS

Defense mechanisms are attempts to defend the individual from anxiety. They are essentially a reaction to frustration - a self-deception.

Causes for Defense Mechanisms

In order to help understand some of the causes for defense mechanisms, remember the basic human needs:

- *Biological or physiological needs* - hunger, water, rest, etc.
- *Psychological or social needs* - status, security, affection, justice etc.

Fear of failure in any of these basic needs appears to be related to the development of defense mechanisms; attitudes toward failure, in turn, originate out of the fabric of childhood experience. The social and cultural conditions encountered during childhood determine the rewards and controls which fill one's later life. These childhood experiences, and their resultant consequences, affect personality development, the individual's value system, and his definition of acceptable goals.

Individuals who are dominated by the fear of failure may react by using one of these defense mechanisms:

- *Rationalization* - making an impulsive action seem logical.

- *Projection* - assigning one's traits to others.

- *Identification* - assuming someone else's favorite qualities are their own.

Results of Use of Defense Mechanisms

A common factor to all defense mechanisms is their quality of *self-deception*. People cling to their impulses and actions, perhaps disguising them so that they become socially acceptable. Their defense mechanisms can be found in the everyday behavior of most normal people and, of course, have *direct influences* on interpersonal relationships.

A person, for example, who is responsible for a particular job makes a mistake, and the work doesn't get done. When confronted with the problem by his supervisor, the individual puts the blame on someone or something else. This is a very common form of a defense mechanism.

Defense mechanisms can sometimes have *negative influences* on interpersonal communications. They can contribute to the individual forming erroneous opinions about the other person's motives. These mechanisms can alter the perceptions and evaluations made about the individual by other people, Ways to understand these mechanisms must be sought; one solution is to become more aware of the common defense mechanisms, and to become less defensive through greater acceptance of others.

5. THE INFLUENCES OF ROLE-PLAYING IN INTERPERSONAL RELATIONS

Everyone wears a mask and plays a certain role or roles in life. Even if the role one plays is to be himself, that particular form of behavior can still be considered a role. As a public-service employee, one's role is to serve the public. This can be done in a number of ways. Some of the factors involved in public-service roles will be mentioned below:

Exploring Superior-Subordinate Relations

Public-service employees are accountable for their actions. From the entry-level public administrative analysis trainee, to the President of the United States, every public servant must be accountable to either an immediate supervisor, a governing body, or to the public itself. Entry-level public-service employees gain experience and get promoted, but they continue to be subordinates and responsible for their actions, even though they also become supervisors and have people working for them.

Simulation exercises can be developed which will examine the perceptions of the superior by the subordinate. *Authority* and *power* factors may enter in here, as the superior also perceives the subordinate in a particular way. *Dominance* and *need* factors are at work in superior-subordinate relationships, and the style of leadership used *(autocratic, democratic,* or *lassiez-faire)* is a form of leadership role.

Peer relationships can be explored through simulation exercises. The ways in which co-workers perceive each other and the resultant effect on cooperation is one area to be examined. Ways to establish a climate or environment for effective, cooperative relations should be sought.

It is desirable also to simulate, for better comprehension, interpersonal communications with the general public. Role-playing techniques, which permit the exploration of person-to-person relationships, are highlighted in the following section on simulation exercises.

Interpersonal Relations Achieved Through Simulation

The preparation of students for entry-level public-service occupations must include an opportunity to experience meaningful interpersonal relations. Public-service employees, whether office or field workers, experience personal relationships with other people every day. The initial success of the public-service worker will depend in large measure upon his ability to interact effectively with others in the office or field. Accordingly, a principle objective of simulation exercises for entry-level public-service education is to have the student acquire the necessary interpersonal relations skills that make for success in all public-service occupations.

When developing a model public-service simulation with the principal objective being to improve favorable interpersonal relations, certain criteria must be established. These criteria may be stated as follows:

- *Interpersonal relations must be the principal component of the simulation*. Provision must be made for students to interact with others in an office interpersonal setting so that they may work and communicate effectively with one another.

- *The simulation must be as realistic as possible*. Realism can best be accomplished by simulating an actual public-service operation in as many areas as possible.

- *Originality must play an important part*. Model simulations, currently in use, must not be copied in an effort to maintain simplicity.

- *The simulation must be interesting*. Students must be motivated to participate in the simulation and to be enthusiastic about its operation.

- *The simulation must be unstructured*. Provision must be made to allow for an awareness of events as they take place. Students must learn to cope with a situation without prior knowledge that the situation will occur.

In order for the teacher to determine if the model public-service simulation developed has, in fact, improved interpersonal relations, the simulation must be evaluated in terms of meeting the established objectives.

6. ## MEASURING INTERPERSONAL RELATIONS
   ### Survey of Interpersonal Values

   A valid and reliable instrument for measuring interpersonal relations, such as the *Survey of Interpersonal Values,* may be used for this purpose. This instrument is intended for grades 9-12, and is designed to measure the relative importance of the major factored interpersonal value dimensions. These values include both the subject's relations with others and others with himself. The value dimensions considered are:

   - *Support*--being treated with understanding, encouragement, kindness, and consideration.

   - *Conformity*--doing what is socially correct, accepted, and proper.

- *Recognition*--being admired, looked up to, considered important, and attracting favorable notice.

- *Independence*--being able to do what one wants to do, making one's own decisions, doing things in one's own way.

- *Benevolence*--doing things for other people, sharing, and helping.

- *Leadership*--being in charge of others, having authority or power.

A pretest on interpersonal values is administered before the model public-service simulation actually begins, and the same test is administerd as a post-test after a stipulated period of time. By comparison of results, and through the use of applicable statistics, the gain in behavior modification in interpersonal relations can be determined, as a result of using the model public-service simulation.

Analysis of Interpersonal Behavior

Public-service employees should be aware of their own needs, and of the needs of other people. They should be able to recognize situations or behavior calling for professional help, and be able to refer people to such appropriate help. New employees must be able to use their knowledge of person-to-person relationships to effectively work with people.

In order to become more effective in interpersonal relationships, students must gain an understanding of:

- *Self-evaluation* - to be able to assess their own strengths and weaknesses.

- *Group Evaluation* - as a class to be able to evaluate other individuals' competencies in interpersonal communications.

- *Correction of own self-perception* - to be able to do something about the knowledge and attitudes formed by adjusting their individual behavior.

STUDENT LEARNING ACTIVITIES

- Define formal and informal social behavior.

- List the important factors in interpersonal communication.

- View and discuss the film strip, *Your Educational Goals, No. 2: Human Relationships.*

- Role play in alternate supervisor-subordinate relationships practicing effective interpersonal communication.

- Write an essay on "Defense mechanisms affect interpersonal relationships."

- View the film, *The Unanswered Question,* and discuss human relationships afterwards.

- Listen to a discussion of structured interpersonal communications and evaluate the effectiveness of the person-to-person relationship.

- In small groups, discuss the ways in which people are mutually dependent on each other,
- Use simulation exercises to practice interpersonal relations.
- List the different kinds of roles and games played in interpersonal communications.
- Debate the statement: *Understanding person-to-person relations is one of the most important skills a person can acquire for success in life.*
- Discuss how understanding interpersonal relationships can help a person to effectively work with people.
- Define the role of recognizing one's own feelings in relation to others.

TEACHER MANAGEMENT ACTIVITIES

- Have the students define formal and informal social behavior.
- Show transparencies on interpersonal relations, *(Social Sensitivity lour Relationship with Others)* and discuss concepts afterwards.
- Assign written exercises on the important factors in interpersonal communication.
- Set up role-playing exercises on subordinate-supervisor roles in effective interpersonal communication.
- Encourage small-group discussions of the ways people are mutually dependent on each other.
- Show a movie on human relationships *(The Unanswered Question)* and discuss key points afterwards.
- Separate the class into teams to debate such statements as: Understanding interpersonal relations is one of the most important skills a person can acquire for success in life.
- Encourage individual study and reading in interpersonal relationships.
- Assign an essay on the worth and dignity of man in interpersonal relations.
- Bring in public-service workers who deal with others to talk to the class about the value of effective interpersonal communications.

10

Evaluation Questions

Fill in the crossword puzzle below.

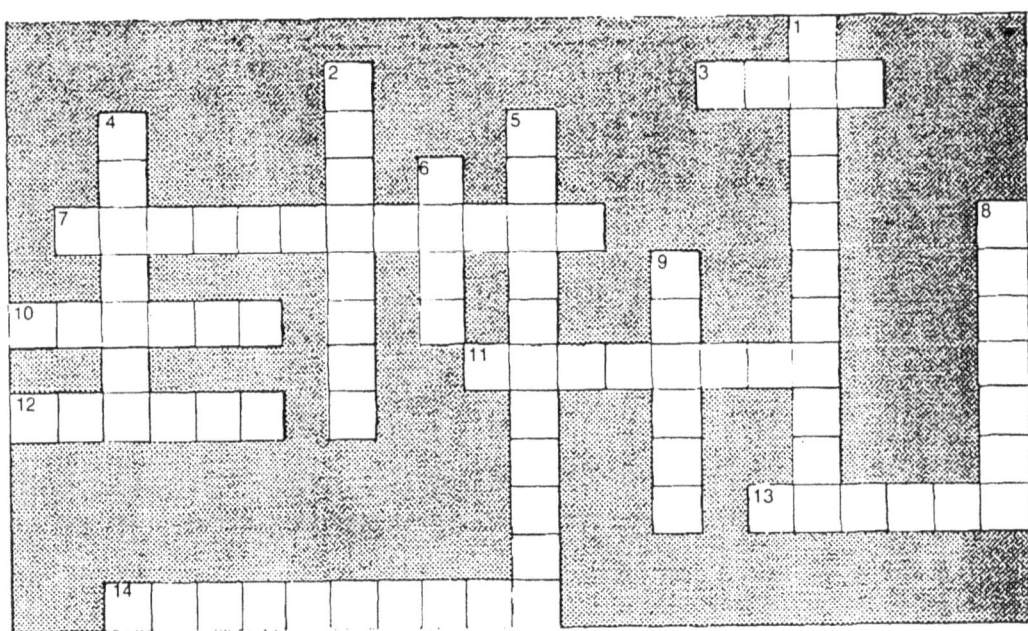

ACROSS:
3. A strong prejudice or _____ can block good relationships.
7. Being able to do what one wants to do satisfies the need for _____.
10. One's _____ of words should be correct for the occasion.
11. Friends usually have an _____ relationship.
12. In talking over problems with others, is important.
13. Everyone needs to feel _____.
14. _____ is assigning one's traits to others.

DOWN:
1. We _____ when we try to make our actions seem logical.
2. When we assume someone's qualities as our own we _____ with that person.
4. Individuals _____ when they do what is socially proper.
5. When we attract favorable attention, we gain _____
6. Some people have a strong _____ of failure.
8. _____ mechanics help to protect a person from anxiety.
9. A public service worker usually has a _____ relationship with the public.

Answer Key

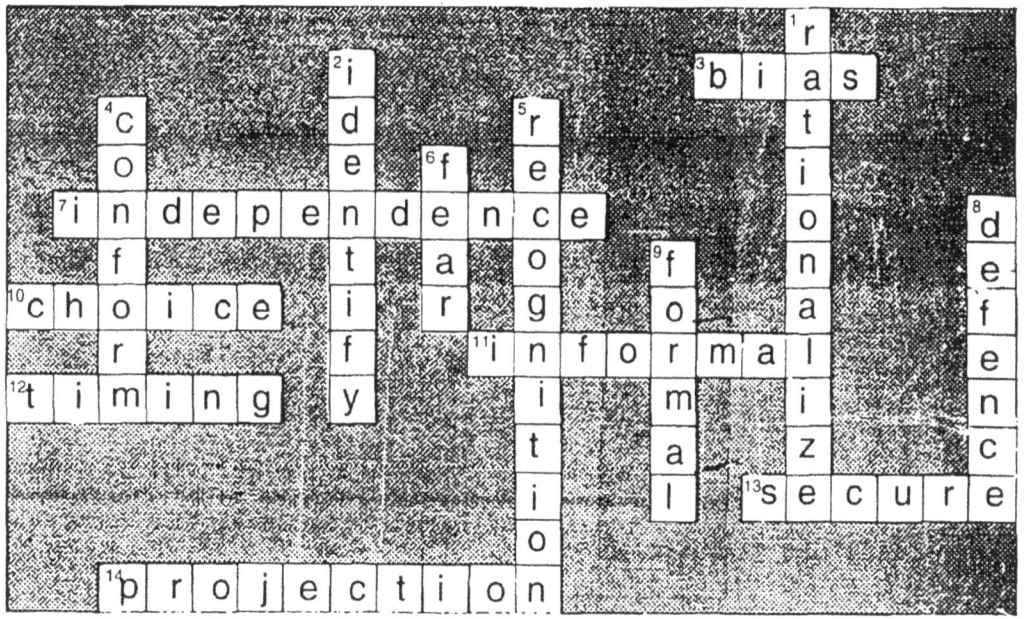

www.ingramcontent.com/pod-product-compliance
Lightning Source LLC
Chambersburg PA
CBHW080736230426
43665CB00020B/2764